LINGUISTICS
The Study of Language

LINGUISTICS
The Study of Language

Chapter Two
of LINGUISTICS
AND
READING

Charles C. Fries
The University of Michigan

Holt, Rinehart and Winston, Inc.
New York   Chicago   San Francisco   Toronto   London

Preface

Just about three hundred years ago, 1660 to be exact, George Fox published his "A Battle-Door for Teachers and Professors to learn Singular and Plural; *You* to Many, and *Thou* to One; Singular One, *Thou;* Plural Many, *You.*"

> Do not they speak false English, false Latin, false Greek . . . and false to the other Tongues, . . . that doth not speak *thou* to *one,* what ever he be, Father, Mother, King, or Judge; is he not a Novice and Unmannerly, and an Ideot and a Fool, that speaks *You* to *one,* which is not to be spoken to a *singular,* but to many? O Vulgar Professors and Teachers, that speaks Plural when they should Singular. . . . Come you Priests and Professors, have you not learned your Accidence?

This change of using the plural forms of the second person pronouns instead of the old singular forms *thou* and *thee,* had by 1660 been in process for more than a hundred years. By the end of the sixteenth century the plural forms *you* or *ye* had become the pronouns for addressing politely but one person. After 1600 the old singular forms *thou* and *thee* gradually disappeared in the ordinary use of English, and, except for religious dialects, *you* became the one form in addressing all ranks of persons.

George Fox's condemnation of this usage constitutes the first clearly stated use in English, so far as I know, of "rules of grammar" ("false English, false Latin, false Greek . . . false to the other Tongues") as a basis for evaluating the language practice of educated people.

A hundred years later, two hundred years ago, such condemnations became very frequent. Robert Lowth (1762) makes a point of stressing what is wrong in the language of "approved authors."

> But let us consider, how, and in what extent, we are to understand this charge brought against the English Language. [Referring to Swift's statement that our language *offends against every part of grammar*]. . . . Does it mean that the English Language, as it is spoken by the politest part of the nation, and as it stands in the writings of our most approved authors, often offends against every part of grammar? Thus far, I am afraid, the charge is true.

James Buchanan (1767) not only condemns the language of approved authors, he also indicates the source of at least part of the criteria for his evaluations.

> Considering the many grammatical Improprieties to be found in our best Writers, such as Swift, Addison, Pope, etc., a Systematical English syntax is not beneath the Notice of the Learned themselves. Should it be urged, that in the Time of these Writers, English was but a very little subjected to Grammar, that they had scarcely a single Rule to direct them, a question readily occurs. Had they not the Rules of Latin Syntax to direct them?

A hundred years after Robert Lowth and James Buchanan, and approximately one hundred years ago, the condemnation of usage, including that of approved authors, is even more specifically announced.

Richard Grant White (1870) *Words and Their Uses:*

> Horace . . . seems to have accepted usage as the supreme authority in speech. . . . But if this dictum were unconditional, and common usage were the absolute and rightful arbiter in all questions of language, there would be no hope of improvement in the speech of an ignorant and degraded society, no rightful protest against its mean and monstrous colloquial phrases, which indeed, would then be neither mean nor monstrous; the fact that they were *in use* being their full justification. The truth is, however, that the authority of general usage, or even of the usage of great writers, is not absolute in language. There is a misuse of words which can be justified by no authority, however great, by no usage, however general. . . .

usage does not justify that which is essentially unreasonable
. . . No amount of wisdom can excuse the use of a really
singular noun with a plural verb, or the reverse.

Even during the last hundred years, the vigorous condemnations of English practice and usage seem to continue the language
attitudes shown in the quotations reaching back to 1670.

> A vast amount of wretched English is heard in this coun-
> try. The remedy does not lie in the repeal of the rules of gram-
> mar; but rather in a stricter and more intelligent enforcement
> of those rules in our schools. . . . Students should be taught
> that correct speaking is evidence of culture; and that in order
> to speak correctly they must master the rules that govern the
> use of the language.

(Editorial, *Detroit Free Press,* December 9, 1928)

> Grammar consists of a series of rules and definitions. . . .
> Since . . . 95 per cent of all children and teachers come from
> homes or communities where incorrect English is used, nearly
> everyone has before him the long, hard task of overcoming
> habits set up early in life before he studied language and gram-
> mar in school. . . . Such people are exposed to the ridicule of
> those who notice the error, and the only way in which they can
> cure themselves is by eternal vigilance and the study of grammar.

(W. W. Charters, *Teaching the Common Branches,* 1924)

And now, in the 1960's, three hundred years after our first
quotation above, the last edition of *Webster's New International
Dictionary* stimulated a large volume of vigorous condemnations
directed especially at the assertion of the editor that "the definitions
are based chiefly on examples of usage" and that the dictionary "is
the record of this language [English] as it is written and spoken."

Concerning this dictionary Jacques Barzun writes in *The
American Scholar,* Spring, 1963

> When it came up as a subject of interest at a meeting of the
> board of *The American Scholar* everyone present felt that its
> importance warranted notice from one of us, and I was dele-
> gated to express the board's "position." . . . none of those
> present had given the new dictionary more than a casual glance,
> yet each one felt that he knew how he stood on the issue that

the work presented to the public. . . . The issue comes down to this: Are the products of the human mind (in this instance language) to be treated like natural objects? The answer Yes means that whatever "the people" utter is a "linguistic fact" to be recorded, cherished, preferred to any reason or tradition.

Although the present-day condemnations of the English language as it appears in the actual practice and usage of English speakers and writers repeat in large part both the attitudes and the vigor of those of earlier years, there is one fundamental difference. The critics of today attempt to put the blame for whatever is wrong with the language upon the "modern linguists" and "modern linguistics."

> For the state of the language as we find it in the centers of culture, certain modern linguists bear a grave responsibility.

(Barzun, *The House of Intellect,* 1959)

> Linguistic scholarship, once an encouragement to the most exacting definitions and standards of workmanship, has for some time been dedicating itself to the abolition of standards; and the new rhetoric evolved under its auspices is an organized assumption that language good enough for anybody is good enough for everybody.

(Wilson Follett, "Grammar is Obsolete," *The Atlantic Monthly,* February 1960)

Some of us who have devoted years to the difficult task of discovering and describing the complicated mechanisms which English actually uses in fulfilling its communicative function, and have struggled hard to understand and to keep abreast of the achievements in modern linguistic science, believe that "linguistics" has much to offer that needs to be explored for help in dealing with the practical problems of learning and teaching.

The content of this little book, *Linguistics: The Study of Language* attempts to survey in non-technical terms the views of the nature and functioning of human language that have gradually emerged as unexpected results of the new techniques and procedures that linguists have used in struggling with problems of language relationship, language history, and descriptive analysis.

This survey of the knowledge and understanding developed over a period of 140 years should help to dispel the "image of the linguist" as one who devotes himself primarily to the destruction of all the qualities that make for precise and full expression—an irresponsible speaker of the language for whom "anything goes." This book should provide answers to such questions as the following.

a) What is the "scientific" study of language or "linguistics" as distinct from the "practical" study of languages?

b) What constitutes the special knowledge that a satisfactorily trained linguist can be expected to bring to his study of language?

c) What criteria must be satisfied in order to produce a linguistically acceptable study based upon "usage."

In other words, what do the actual publications of recognized "linguists" reveal concerning the aims of their work, the materials which they study, and the criteria of success or achievement by which their profession evaluates the results.

The material reproduced here constitutes Chapter 2 of the book *Linguistics and Reading*—a book which attempts to explore the applications of linguistic knowledge and understanding to the many complex problems of teaching reading. This chapter is here issued as a separate unit in response to many requests to make this brief survey easily available for other purposes.

Charles C. Fries

Philadelphia
May 1964

Contents

Linguistics: The Study of Language

For many of those who deal with the practical problems of the schools and for the general public the word *linguistics* has the ring of something quite new. It seems to stand for something that has grown up very recently—something radical. On the other hand, there are those who understand *linguistics* as simply a new label for the familiar struggle to learn foreign languages. To them a *linguist* is one who can speak several languages. To be a "good linguist" for a large part of even the well-educated public means to speak foreign languages fluently.

Linguistics, however, in the special sense of that word as used in the title of this book and of this chapter, does not concern itself primarily with the practical study of languages. Linguists do study languages. Good linguists find it necessary to study a great variety of languages—especially languages that differ fundamentally in structure from their own native language. But this study of languages by "linguists" does not have as its primary aim and purpose the building up of the habits of use required to speak them fluently or even well enough to communicate through reading or writing. Most "linguists" study languages in order to know and to understand their structures—the particular ways in which these languages use their linguistic units to achieve their communicative function. They seek primarily, knowledge *about* the units and the working processes of each language, rather than the ability to speak them. Of course, some linguists, like Bloomfield and the workers of the Summer Institute of Linguistics, do strive to learn to speak the languages they set out to describe scientifically. The linguist, as linguist, however, studies a wide variety of languages because he seeks primarily to understand *the processes of human language*. He is somewhat like the zoologist, who studies animal life in a wide variety of forms—from protozoa to vertebrates. He is perhaps more like the anthropologist, who studies the life of humans in a great variety of the groups of mankind. In other words, a linguist is a "scientist" whose field of research and knowledge is human language, not the practical mastery of languages. Languages constitute the specific material upon which he works, but through the concrete evidence of the workings of each of these languages the linguistic scientist tries to understand the nature of human language and the processes of its functioning. The fruit of his work constitutes "linguistic science."

The special way in which the linguistic scientist studies languages to achieve his purpose we shall call here the "scientific study of language" or *linguistics,* and use the phrase "the practical study of languages" whenever we wish to designate that language study which seeks to master one or more languages for practical use.

This "scientific study of language" is not very new. It seems new to many people because only comparatively recently have vigorous popular discussions used the particular terms "linguist," "linguistics," and the "scientific study of language." In most of these recent popular discussions, the more than a century-long history of this type of study is not only never mentioned but the views attributed to linguists are often attacked as the private theories of a small group of radicals devoted to a program of undermining the defenses of "accurate and elegant expression."[1] But modern linguistics, as the scientific study of language through the work of a great host of linguistic scholars, has, since the first quarter of the nineteenth century, built up a tremendous body of new knowledge concerning the nature and functioning of human language which has not yet been assimilated by or even known to the general public.

It is true that the knowledge so gained has made it necessary for linguists to abandon many of the traditional views of language vigorously set forth in the seventeenth and eighteenth centuries, especially those dominating the grammars and dictionaries of the second half of the eighteenth century—the English grammars of Archbishop Lowth, of William Ward, of Charles Coote, and of Lindley Murray, and the dictionaries of Samuel Johnson, and of Thomas Sheridan. But linguists have abandoned these conventional views not because of any deliberate purpose on their part to oppose the conventional views but because their use of the newer methods of language study forced them to conclusions that made the traditional views of language untenable.

LINGUISTIC SCIENCE FROM 1820 TO 1875

It is, of course, quite arbitrary to fix a precise date for the "beginning" of any significant intellectual advance. The best we can do is to place in time some specific evidence of a breakthrough into the new ways of working and the new understandings upon which later scholars have built. In linguistics such a breakthrough into a new way of studying the problems of language diversity and relationship occurred with the publication in 1818 of Erasmus Rask's *Investigation on the Origin of the Old Norse or Icelandic Language*[2] and the publication of the second edition of the first volume of Jakob Grimm's *Deutsche Grammatik* in 1822. These two publications started a succession of workers upon a long series of studies that had the two fundamental characteristics of a science—that it be *cumulative* and *impersonal*. It must be *cumulative* in the sense that all contributions must build upon, or take cognizance of, all that has preceded; and *impersonal* in the sense that the techniques used must lead to generalizations that are verifiable by all competent persons.[3] To be "science" the results obtained cannot remain private theories perpetuated by authority.

The scientific study of language has had since 1825 a host of devoted workers building upon, refining, and extending the techniques that proved most productive of verifiable conclusions. From time to time linguistic scholars have tried to summarize for the general public the results of this scientific study of language.

During the month of March 1863, Professor William Dwight Whitney of Yale University delivered six lectures "On the Principles of Linguistic Science" at the Smithsonian Institution in Washington, D.C. A brief abstract of these lectures was printed in the Institution's Annual Report.[4] These lectures were expanded to twelve and delivered before the Lowell Institute in Boston in December 1864 and January 1865. Rewritten and expanded again, they were published in 1867 in a book of 505 pages under the title *Language and the Study of Language: Twelve Lectures on the Principles of Linguistic Science*. Their substance constituted the basis of his "instruction in the science of language" in Yale University. Professor Whitney believed

. . . that at least so much knowledge of the nature, history, and classifications of language as is here presented ought to be included in every scheme of higher education, even for those who do not intend to become special students in comparative philology. Much more necessary, of course, is it to those who cherish such intention. It is, I am convinced, a mistake to commence at once upon a course of detailed comparative philology with pupils who have only enjoyed the training in the classical or the modern languages or in both. They are liable either to fail of apprehending the value and interest of the infinity of particulars into which they are plunged, or else to become wholly absorbed in them, losing sight of the grand truths and principles which underlie and give significance to their work, and the recognition of which ought to govern its course throughout.[5]

Invited to contribute a volume on language to *The International Scientific Series,* begun in London in 1873, Whitney produced his *Life and Growth of Language: An Outline of Linguistic Science,* a book of 327 pages, in 1875. Several of the comments from his introductory chapter should be added to the statements quoted from his earlier book.

Yet the body of truth [concerning the general problems of language] has been so small, that the science of language is to be regarded as a modern one, as much so as geology and chemistry; it belongs like them to the nineteenth century. . . . Although of so recent growth, the science of language is already one of the leading branches of modern inquiry. It is not less comprehensive in its material, definite in its aims, strict in its methods, and rich and fruitful in its results, than its sister sciences. Its foundations have been laid deep and strong in the thorough analysis of many of the most important human tongues, and the careful examination and classification of nearly all the rest. It has yielded to the history of mankind as a whole, and to that of the different races of men, definite truths and far-reaching glimpses of truth which could be won in no other way. It is bringing about a recast of the old methods of teaching even familiar and long-studied languages, like the Latin and Greek; it is drawing forward to conspicuous notice others of which, only a few years ago, hardly the names were known. It has, in short, leavened all the connected branches of knowledge and worked itself into the very structure of modern thought, so that no one who hears or reads can help taking some cognizance of it. No educated person can afford to lack a clear conception of at least a brief connected outline of a science possessing such claims to attention. The design of this volume, accordingly, is to draw out and illustrate the principles of linguistic science, and to set forth its results, with as much fullness as the limited space at command shall allow.[6]

Especially significant was Whitney's clear-sighted grasp of the distinction to be made between the building up of an extensive body of exact information concerning a wide range of different languages and the conclusions relating to the nature and functioning of language to be derived from this information—the conclusions which constitute the heart and substance of linguistic science.

Comparative philology and linguistic science, we may say, are two sides of the same study: the former deals primarily with the individual facts of a certain body of languages, classifying them, tracing out their relations, and arriving at the conclusions they suggest; the latter makes the laws and general principles of speech its main subject, and uses particular facts rather as illustrations. The one is the working phase, the other the regulative and critical and teaching phase of the science. The one is more important as a part of special training, the other as an element of general culture—if, indeed, it be proper to raise any question as to their relative importance, even to the special student of language; for the lack of either will equally unfit him for doing the soundest and best service. . . .

Yet the two are certainly different enough to make it possible that a scholar should excel in the one and not in the other. The science of language runs out, on its comparative side, into an infinity of details, like chemistry or zoölogy; and one may be extremely well versed in the manipulation of its special processes while wholly wrong as regards its grander generalizations: just as one may be a skillful analyst while knowing little or nothing of the philosophy of chemistry, or eminent in the comparative anatomy of animals with no sound knowledge or judgment as to the principles of biology. To illustrate this, it would be easy to cite remarkable examples of men of the present generation, enjoying high distinction as comparative philologists, who, as soon as they attempt to reason on the wider truths of linguistic science, fall into incongruities and absurdities; or, in matters of minor importance, they show in manifold ways the lack of a sound and defensible basis of general theoretical views. Comparative work of the broadest scope and greatest value has long been done and is still doing; but the science of language is only in the most recent period taking shape; and its principles are still subjects of great diversity of opinion and of lively controversy. It is high time that this state of things, tolerable only in the growing and shaping period of study, should come to an end, and that, as in other sciences of observation and deduction—for example, in chemistry, zoölogy, geology—there should be acknowledged to exist a body, not of facts only, but of truths, so well established that he who rejects them shall have no claim to be considered a man of science.[7]

These two books by Whitney on the principles and results of "linguistic science" appeared in 1867 and in 1875, nearly a century ago, but almost fifty years after the first breakthrough in the struggle to find sound techniques by which to explore and establish the relationships of diverse languages. Before 1818, questions concerning language—of origin, of diversity, of relationship, of structure, of meaning—were approached primarily through speculation and appeals to authority.[8] The fifty years from the linguistic ground-breaking of Rask and Grimm to the publication of Whitney's books saw the development of a considerable body of verifiable knowledge concerning language, built up through the use of techniques accessible to all who would become proficient workers in linguistics. The special technique from which the first steps in modern linguistic science started was based upon correspondences of sounds.

Rask and Grimm, by means of the law of Lautverschiebung [sound change, or the Law of Permutation of Consonants] established the fact that the changes of sounds, or as it was then expressed, of *letters,* into one another take place in accordance with laws, and above all, that a fixed historical relation can be observed between the sounds of the German on the one side and of the classical languages on the other. . . .

[This law] . . . goes by Grimm's name, although already pro-claimed by Rask in its main features.[9]

With Rask, this phonological technique was generalized as the means of exploring and proving a genetic relationship between any languages, and it became the firm basis for establishing language "families." Rask's statement, in translation, follows.

A language, however mixed it may be, belongs to the same branch of languages as another when it has the most essential, concrete, indispensable words, the foundation of the language, in common with it. . . . When agreement is found in such words . . . , and so frequently that rules may be drawn up for the shift in letters from one to the other, then there is a fundamental relationship between the two languages. . . .[10]

This principle of rules for the "correspondences in the shift of sounds" or "laws of sound change" provided the beginnings of a new and scientific approach to etymology and the ground upon which to repudiate conclusions based on chance likenesses. It furnished a criterion from which to evaluate both the evidence and the conclusions concerning linguistic relationships. Linguistics thus began to achieve the status of a "science" with the developing of the techniques and procedures for identifying and analyzing the linguistic evidence significant for determining the genetic relationship (or non-relationship) of diverse languages. The developing of these techniques and procedures throughout the fifty years from 1820 to 1875 was the cumulative contribution of an increasing body of workers. As Whitney expressed it in 1867,

A host of worthy rivals and followers of the men whose names we have noted [Rask, Bopp, Grimm, Pott, Burnouf] have arisen in all parts of Europe and even in America, to continue the work which those had begun; and by their aid the science has already attained a degree of advancement that is truly astonishing considering its recent origin.[11]

Whitney also indicated something of the breadth of the field of linguistics:

The material and subject of linguistic science is language, in its entirety; all the accessible forms of human speech, in their infinite variety, whether still living in the minds and mouths of men, or preserved only in written documents, or carved on the scantier but more imperishable records of brass and stone. It has a field and scope limited to no age, and to no portion of mankind. The dialects of the obscurest and most humbly endowed races are its care, as well as those of leaders in the world's history. Whenever and wherever a sound has dropped from the lips of a human being, to signalize to others the movement of his spirit, this science would fain take it up and study it, as having a character and office worthy of attentive examination. Every fact of every language, in the view of the linguistic student, calls for his investigation, since only in the light of all can any be completely understood. To assemble, arrange, and explain the whole body of linguistic phenomena, so as thoroughly to comprehend them, in each separate part and under all aspects, is his endeavor.[12]

Thus even during the first fifty years the scientific study of language was not narrowly conceived. The heart and substance of the linguistic science of even this first period of its development was not simply in its new tools of operation but rather in the growing understanding of the nature of language itself. This growing understanding of certain basic characteristics of language did not, in most instances, come as the conclusions of conscious inquiry into these characteristics, but rather as the *unexpected results* of the use of the new linguistic techniques and procedures as applied to the study of a great variety of languages. Some of the basic characteristics of language that have thus formed part of the knowledge that constituted the linguistic science of this period are the following:

(1) All living language is in a condition of constant growth and change. It matters not to what part of the world we may go: if we find for any existing speech a record of its predecessor at some time distant from it in the past, we shall perceive that the two are different—and more or less different, mainly in proportion to the distance in time that separates them. . . . An English speaker even of only a century ago would find not a little in our every-day speech which he would understand with difficulty, or not at all; if we were to hear Shakespeare read aloud a scene from one of his own works, it would be in no small part unintelligible. . . . Chaucer's English (500 years ago) we master by dint of good solid application, and with considerable help from a glossary; and King Alfred's English (1000 years ago), which we call Anglo-Saxon, is not easier to us than German. All this, in spite of the fact that no one has gone about of set purpose to alter English speech, in any generation among the thirty or forty that have lived between us and Alfred, any more than in our own. Here, then, is another side of the life of language for us to deal with, and to explain, if we can.[13]

(2) Language and dialect . . . are only two names for the same thing, as looked at from different points of view. Any body of expressions used by a community, however limited and humble, for the purposes of communication and as the instrument of thought, is a language; no one would think of crediting its speakers with the gift of dialect but not of language. On the other hand, there is no tongue in the world to which we should not with perfect freedom and perfect propriety apply the name of dialect, when considering it as one of a body of related forms of speech. The science of language has democratized our views on such points as these; it has taught us that one man's speech is just as much a language as another man's; that even the most cultivated tongue that exists is only the dialect of a certain class in a certain locality—both class and locality limited, though the limits may be wide ones. The written English is one of the forms of English, used by the educated class for certain purposes, having dialectic characters by which it is distinguished from the colloquial speech of the same class, and yet more from the speech of other classes or sections of the English-speaking community—and each one of these is as valuable to the comparative student of language as their alleged superior. But English and Dutch and German and Swedish, and so on, are the dialects of Germanic speech; and the same, along with French and Irish and Bohemian, and the rest, are dialects of the wider family whose limits we have drawn above. This is the scientific use of the terms. . . .[14]

(3) The constant changes in language are not corruptions that can or should be eliminated or prevented. The actual changing usage of people constitutes the basis of all the "correctness" there can be in language, and the facts upon which to state the history of a language. There can be no other approach upon which to build a scientific history of a language. It was in this first period of the development of linguistic science that the two great historical dictionaries were begun. The collecting of the evidence for the *Deutsches Wörterbuch* began in 1837 and that for the *Oxford English Dictionary* (earlier called *A New English Dictionary on Historical Principles*) was undertaken in 1858. For the *Oxford English Dictionary* the editing, under the direction of Sir James Murray, started in 1878, twenty years after the collecting began. The first part was published in 1884 and the first volume in 1888. The final part came from the press in 1928, seventy years after the collecting started. This dictionary set out to do, and actually accomplished, the most complete survey of usage ever attempted in any language. Altogether the editors of the *Oxford English Dictionary* had in hand, as the basis for their conclusions, more than

six million dated quotations with exact references to their place of occurrence so that they could each be verified. The following two excerpts from the Preface to the first edition of Volume I of that dictionary give the first editor's own statement of their aim and approach.

It was proposed that materials should be collected for a Dictionary which, by the completeness of its vocabulary, and by the application of the historical method to the life and use of words, might be worthy of the English language and of English scholarship. With this view, it was resolved to begin at the beginning, and extract anew typical quotations for the use of words, from all the great English writers of all ages, and from all writers on special subjects whose works might illustrate the history of words employed in special senses, from all writers whatever before the 16th century, and from as many as possible of the more important writers of later times.

The aim of this Dictionary is to furnish an adequate account of the meaning, origin, and history of English words now in general use, or known to have been in use at any time during the last seven hundred years. It endeavours (1) to show, with regard to each individual word, when, how, in what shape, and with what signification, it became English; what development of form and meaning it has since received; which of its uses have, in the course of time, become obsolete, and which still survive; what new uses have since arisen, by what processes, and when; (2) to illustrate these facts by a series of quotations ranging from the first known occurrence of the word to the latest, or down to the present day; the word being thus made to exhibit its own history and meaning; and (3) to treat the etymology of each word strictly on the basis of historical fact, and in accordance with the methods and results of modern philological [linguistic] science.[15]

Although the editing of the *Oxford English Dictionary* lasted through the whole of the second period of the development of linguistic science, it can, in respect to its principles and design, still be regarded as one of the products of the linguistic achievements of the years from 1820 to 1875. The producing of such a dictionary was discussed during the years before 1858, when the collection of materials was formally undertaken by The Philological Society.[16] The basic design of the use of these materials and the statement of the aims of the *Oxford Dictionary* stemmed directly from the new linguistic approach here discussed. It thus differed fundamentally from that of Dr. Samuel Johnson (1755) which had become the model for all succeeding commercial dictionaries, even those of recent times. Johnson's *Dictionary* very clearly rested upon and in itself supported the views of the nature and functioning of language that dominated the second half of the eighteenth century. The *Oxford English Dictionary,* which was planned and undertaken a century later, rested upon and became an important tool in the application of the startlingly new views of the nature and functioning of language that began to arise out of the very different techniques and procedures of the linguistic work from 1820 to 1875.

Johnson's *Dictionary* depended on and attached to the lexicographical work of Nathaniel Bailey (especially the second edition of Bailey's *Dictionary* of 1730). Bailey, for example, was the first of the completely English dictionaries (that is, English dictionaries for English people as distinct from two-language dictionaries) to try to include the whole English vocabulary. The preceding English dictionaries had confined themselves to the "hard" words, especially those borrowed from Latin and Greek. Bailey first included words like *cat, dog,* and *horse.* Johnson followed Bailey in this feature as have the "unabridged" dictionaries following him. The *Oxford English Dictionary,* however, from its much more thorough survey of usage, records six times as many vocabulary entries as does Johnson.

In a feature that differed from Bailey, Johnson first consistently gave quotations from English literature to illustrate the meanings which he described in the definitions. These quotations, however, served merely as illustrations and were not designed to furnish the evidence for his explanations and comments as shown by the fact that in many instances the comments contradict the evidence furnished by the quotations.

The third special feature of Johnson's *Dictionary* is of particular concern for our discussion here. In this dictionary, as editor, Johnson gave judgments concerning the status of the forms, the meanings, and the uses of many of the vocabulary items he included.[17] In a considerable number of instances Johnson condemns words and expressions for which he gives quotations showing their use in English literature by generally approved authors. It is in this feature especially that Johnson became the "father" of most of the later commercial dictionaries. Four examples of such judgments follow.

For the word *budge,* he gives as definition "To stir, to move off the place," and then, in spite of two quotations from Shakspere and one from Samuel Butler's *Hudibras,* he calls it "a low word."

For *fun,* he quotes from Moore and defines it as "Sport; high merriment; frolicsome delight," but calls it "a low cant word."

For *clever* he gives three separate definitions,—(1) "dextrous; skilful," (2) "just; fit; proper; commodious," (3) "well shaped; handsome"—with quotations from L'Estrange, Addison, Pope, and Arbuthnot. Then his judgment follows: "This is a low word, scarcely ever used but in burlesque or conversation; and applied to anything a man likes, without settled meaning."

For *excepting,* in spite of quotations from Dryden and Collier, he calls it "an improper word."

In contrast with this typical eighteenth-century authoritarian attitude toward language, the *Oxford English Dictionary* as a matter of principle gives no such status judgments. It presents a selection of the significant evidence, from the dated quotations collected, as the ground for the conclusions concerning the history of each word and of its various meanings in English. The "definitions" simply state the conclusions that can be drawn from the evidence in hand. In Johnson's *Dictionary* and in others the definitions and comments of the editors are the important matter; they often go beyond or even contradict the illustrative quotations. The *Oxford Dictionary* treatment of the word *nice* represents the new view of language. There is no condemnation of any of the ways in which the word *nice* has been used since its first introduction into the English language in the latter part of the thirteenth century. The editors give the quotations that show that it came into English from Old French, with the meaning of foolish, stupid, senseless (Latin *nescius,* ignorant). It passed through several developments of meaning: "wanton, loose-mannered"; "slothful, lazy, indolent"; "coy, shy, reserved"; "fastidious, dainty, hard to please"; "strict, careful"; "requiring or involving great precision"; "minutely or carefully accurate"; and then our modern common use, "agreeable, that one derives pleasure or satisfaction from, delightful"; "a general epithet of approval." The *Oxford Dictionary* shows that this meaning of *general approval* has been attached to the word *nice,* and has appeared in our literature with that meaning, ever since the middle of the eighteenth century.

By 1875, the end of the first fifty years of this "modern scientific study" of language, the following views of language became for linguists the ground upon which they based their procedures.

(1) Constant change is to be expected in all languages at every period of their history. It was these changes that formed the object of study.

(2) These changes are not a succession of unrelated events in which anything can happen at random. These changes, in spite of what seemed to be many exceptions, showed a surprising regularity. They showed so much regularity, in fact, that it was possible to grasp this regularity in generalizations upon which to determine language relationships, and to establish "families" of languages. This assumption of basic regularity of change made possible scientific linguistic investigation.

(3) These changes of language could not have been the result of corruptions arising out of the mistakes of the ignorant or the careless. Only by assuming that the usage of the speakers and writers of a language is the only basis of "correctness" could such a dictionary as the *Oxford English Dictionary* have been produced. The editorial work upon this dictionary was preceded (beginning in 1858) by a tremendous labor of collecting the evidence for the facts of usage.

LINGUISTIC SCIENCE FROM 1875 TO 1925

But the achievements in linguistic science, the new views of the nature and functioning of language arising unexpectedly out of the broadening use of the new techniques for the study of language, as discussed in Whitney's two books, constitute only the first steps in the development of linguistics. A second breakthrough into new understanding concerning our knowledge of language occurred in the 1870s with the publishing of a series of brilliant articles solv-

ing the problems arising out of the large number of seeming ir-
regularities or "exceptions" to the sound-laws postulated for the
Indo-European family of languages.

"Phonetic Laws Without Exceptions"

We would mark the beginning of the second period of linguistic science, again a span of about fifty years, with the publishing of
Karl Verner's paper[18] establishing what has been called "Verner's
Law of Accent." It was one of a number of papers dealing with the
apparent exceptions to the "sound-laws" (the generalizations concerning correspondences of forms) that had been established for
the Indo-European family of languages. Verner's article disposed
of the greatest body of "exceptions" to the Germanic sound-
shift.

> . . . the effect of Verner's article . . . was immeasurable. Now there were
> no more exceptions to the Germanic sound-shift, and this absence of
> exceptions necessarily had quite as strong an effect upon the whole
> conception of linguistics as the chief laws applying to the sound-shifts
> had exerted in their time. Then, scholars were beginning to understand
> that there were laws of phonology; now, they were awaking to the
> fact that such laws operate regularly [or without exception].[19]

As Verner expressed it in 1875, "There must be a rule for
irregularity; the problem is to find it." Or as he had earlier phrased
the general principle, in 1872, "No exception without a rule."[20]

But Karl Verner, a Dane, was not alone in building the evidence that now induced linguists "to postulate complete adherence
to laws in the development of sounds," and to seek a scientifically
verifiable explanation for every deviation. Others made notable
contributions, including Graziadio Ascoli, an Italian; August Les-
kien and Karl Brugmann, both Germans; and the French Swiss
Ferdinand de Saussure.

It became clear, however, that, although in the mass of
changes to be observed in languages through a period of time,
phonological changes were fundamental for a scientific approach,
yet there were other changes that lay outside the area of sound-
changes. The more rigorously linguistic scholars sought the sup-
plementary sound laws that would explain the residues of exceptions to the generalizations tentatively set up, the more precisely

they could identify and isolate the portions of these residues for which other types of explanation were necessary. Two kinds of changes other than sound-changes were now recognized:

(a) those that came about through *analogical creation,* and
(b) those that arose through *borrowings* from other languages and dialects.

Analogical Creation

Through *analogical creation,* or *levelling,* new forms were brought into line with some pattern that for some reason had become especially strong. For example, of the nouns in Old English, only masculine "*-a* stems" like *stān* (Modern English *stōne*) had an "*s*"-form plural, *stānas.* This pattern of an "*s*" form for the plural gradually supplanted other forms for the plural, until now in Modern English, less than five percent of the nouns, even in running discourse, have plural forms other than "*s*"[21]: *boy - boys; bed - beds; rock - rocks; bush - bushes; church - churches; judge - judges.* This so-called *s*-form plural became such a strong pattern that nearly all foreign words, even those borrowed from Greek and Latin, have now regular "*s*" plurals; as, for example, *ideas, families, sciences, operas, formulas.*

These changes have come about through the process of *analogy,* not through the processes of a sound-change that can be grasped by the kind of generalization that constitutes a *phonetic law.* The recognition of the principle of analogy, together with the effort to treat analogy rigorously, helped to remove one large body of the "exceptional" forms that made up the residues not explained by the accepted sound-laws.

Borrowings

The recognition of the fact that sound-laws operated within a certain period of time and within a particular language or dialect also made it possible to remove "borrowed" words from the body of what seemed to be exceptions. For example, although our word *kitchen* (Old English *cycena*) appears even in Old English texts, it is not a native English word, cognate with Latin *coquina.* If it were it would be an exception to Grimm's Law of Consonant Shift. It was borrowed from Latin long after the period of the operation of the Germanic sound-change (Grimm's Law) and therefore has the same initial consonant it had in Latin. But the borrowing must have occurred before the operation of the prehistoric English sound-change called "i-umlaut," for only in this way can one account for the particular change of vowel from the Latin [o] to English [ɪ] in the first syllable. Thus borrowed words, through the evidence of their sound features reveal not only the fact that they are borrowed and not native, but also something of the time at which they were borrowed.

The assumptions concerning the nature of human language that grew out of the more rigorous treatment of sound-change, supplemented with new insights into the processes of analogical creation and borrowing, marked the special growth of linguistic science in the latter part of the nineteenth century. The acceptance of the strict "regularity" of sound-change became general in linguistic science—acceptance not as a dogma of belief, but as a basic assumption that has proved most productive in practice. The principle of "regularity" in language change—so regular that from adequately stated generalizations linguistic predictions have been possible—also provided the ground upon which to evaluate both the evidence and the conclusions of linguistic studies.

Linguistics may be said to have begun its scientific career with the comparative study and reconstruction of the Indo-European languages. In the course of their detailed researches Indo-European linguists have gradually developed a technique which is probably more nearly perfect than that of any other science dealing with man's institutions. Many of the formulations of comparative Indo-European linguistics have a neatness and a regularity which recall the formulae, or the so-called laws, of natural science. . . .

The methods developed by the Indo-Europeanists have been applied with marked success to other groups of languages. It is abundantly clear that they apply as rigorously to the unwritten primitive languages of Africa and America as to the better known forms of speech of the more sophisticated peoples. . . . The more we devote ourselves to the comparative study of the languages of a primitive linguistic stock, the more clearly we realize that phonetic law and analogical leveling are the only satisfactory key to the unravelling of the development of dialects and languages from a common base. Professor Leonard Bloomfield's experience with Central Algonkian and my own with Athabaskan leave nothing to be desired in this respect and are a complete answer to those who find it difficult to accept the large scale regularity of the operation of all those unconscious linguistic forces which in their totality give us regular phonetic change and morphological readjustment on the basis of such a change. It is not merely theoretically possible to predict the correctness of specific forms among unlettered peoples on the basis of such phonetic laws as have been worked out for them—such predictions are already on record in considerable number.[22]

The following statement attempts to summarize briefly the chief features of what is meant by the heading of this section— "Phonetic Laws Without Exceptions."

From evidence such as the following,

(a) correspondences in the representations of certain words in several languages,
(b) certain changes in the representations of the same word in the records of the same language separated by a period of time,

we infer that there was a change in the native speaker's manner of pronouncing a particular "sound," and that this change

(1) affected every occurrence of that "sound" in essentially the same phonetic surroundings,

(2) operated within a particular span of time and within a particular dialect or group of dialects,

(3) was not interfered with by any nonphonetic factors such as meaning, homonymy, etc.

Statements of such changes have often been called "phonetic laws." They are rather descriptive generalizations of the observed correspondences of forms, the result of historical change. They do not set forth the processes of these changes nor indicate their causes. By assumption, these descriptive generalizations, if they are accurately and completely stated, must apply "without exception" to the whole body of the "native" words of a language, or a dialect or a group of dialects. Whatever residues there may be must be strictly accounted for by the processes of analogy or borrowing.

In addition to this major linguistic contribution leading to a practical understanding of the assumption of "Phonetic Laws Without Exceptions," two other linguistic developments of the period from 1875 to 1925 need brief comment before concluding this section. They are linguistic geography and phonetics.

Linguistic Geography

The increasing number of studies in the history of a variety of languages brought to light more and more evidence that the "standard" language, or the prestige form of a language, had, because of particular historical circumstances, arisen out of the dialects, rather than that the dialects had diverged from the "standard" language. "Standard" English, for example, arose out of the old dialect of London, as that speech gained more and more prestige when London, in the fourteenth century, became increasingly the center of affairs for a more unified England. The divergent linguistic forms of the speech of other dialects were not, as was earlier believed, corrupted forms derived through ignorance or carelessness from those of standard or literary English. In many instances these divergent forms proved to be older. The efforts to understand the relationships of dialect to standard language and dialect to dialect led again to the gathering and recording of these facts of usage in dialect dictionaries, dialect grammars, and the assortment of maps that constitute a dialect atlas. As Whitney had insisted in 1867

The material and subject of linguistic science is language, in its entirety. . . . The dialects of the obscurest and most humbly endowed races are its care, as well as those of leaders in the world's history. . . . Every fact of every language, in the view of the linguistic student, calls for his investigation, *since only in the light of all can any be completely understood.* [The italics are mine.][23]

The period from 1875 to 1925 saw an increasing variety of language and dialect surveys with constant improvements in the techniques of making the surveys and interpreting the data. Of these, the following are the best-known examples:

Georg Wenker in 1876 began the work which led to the *Sprachatlas des deutschen Reichs.*

Jules Gilliéron planned and edited the *Atlas linguistique de la France* (1902–1908) based on the survey material gathered by Edmond Edmont.

K. Jaberg and J. Jud began the publication of the *Sprach- und Sachatlas Italiens und Südschweiz* in 1928, just when the formal collecting of material began for the *Linguistic Atlas of the United States and Canada.*[24]

Linguistic geography thus supplemented language history in leading to a much clearer understanding of the significance of dialect differences in a language, of the centers of language dispersion, and of the basis for the special prestige through which one regional dialect out of many becomes a "standard" language.

Phonetics

It is not surprising that "phonetics" should have had an especially vigorous development during the years from 1875 to 1925. The generalizations upon which the "new" linguistic science was founded were generalizations concerning the sounds of the languages. It was the sound-changes of language that were especially stable, and sound-changes rather than grammatical changes that showed amazing regularity. To understand all that could be learned concerning the nature of speech sounds, therefore, became quite naturally one of the flourishing major interests. Phonetics as the science of speech sounds[25] began to develop new techniques for the analysis and description of the sounds of all languages. *Articulatory phonetics* had growing success in attempting to analyze and describe the physical movements by which speech sounds are differentiated. *Instrumental phonetics,* beginning with the simple laryngoscope, the x-ray, and the false palate, to increase the range of direct observation, advanced to more complex devices like the kymograph and the oscillograph to study the physical or acoustic properties of sounds and to "photograph" them. Out of this increasing study of speech sounds came the realization that there are a great many more differences of sound used, even in our own native language, than we had thought possible.

The feeling that the average speaker has of his language is that it is built up, acoustically speaking, of a comparatively small number of distinct sounds, each of which is rather accurately provided for in the current alphabet by one letter or, in a few cases, by two or more alternative letters. As for the languages of foreigners, he generally feels that, aside from a few striking differences that cannot escape even the uncritical ear, the sounds they use are the same as those he is familiar with but that there is a mysterious "accent" to these foreign languages, a certain unanalyzed phonetic character, apart from the sounds as such, that gives them their air of strangeness. This naïve feeling is largely illusory on both scores.[26]

G. B. Shaw's well-known *Pygmalion* (1900)[26a] makes dramatic use of some of the enormous number of phonetic differences in the various kinds of pronunciation of English. Higgins, the phonetician in the play, says,

You can spot an Irishman or a Yorkshireman by his brogue. *I* can place any man within six miles. I can place him within two miles in London. Sometimes within two streets.

Of the Flower Girl, Higgins says,

You see this creature with her kerbstone English: the English that will keep her in the gutter to the end of her days. Well, sir, in three months I could pass that girl off as a duchess at an ambassador's garden party. I could even get her a place as lady's maid or shop assistant, which requires better English.

Later he asks Pickering (a phonetician of ability but of somewhat less skill):

HIGGINS: Tired of listening to sounds?
PICKERING: Yes. It's a fearful strain. I rather fancied myself because I can pronounce twenty-four distinct vowel sounds; but your hundred and thirty beat me. I can't hear a bit of difference between most of them.
HIGGINS: Oh, that comes with practice. You hear no difference at first; but you keep on listening, and presently you find they're all as different as A and B.

Not only did the analyses of the phoneticians bring to light and describe the tremendous number of differences of vocal sounds that appear in a language like English—differences of sound of which the native speakers are not aware, except as broad differences of "accent"—but they required a greatly increased set of graphic symbols in order to pin them down and discuss them.

HIGGINS. . . . I'll show you how I make records. We'll set her [the Flower Girl] talking; and I'll take it down first in Bell's Visible Speech; then in broad Romic; then we'll get her on the phonograph so that you can turn her on as often as you like with the written transcript before you.

In the quotation from *Pygmalion* just given Higgins suggests that he will "write down" the Flower Girl's pronunciation exactly, so that the "written transcript" can be compared with the actual sounds recorded on the phonograph. The conversation just preceding had already indicated that Pickering could distinguish 24 different vowel sounds and that Higgins could identify 130. The writing proposed must therefore have available sufficient distinctly different letters (or symbols) to record these differences. At the opening of the play the Note Taker (Higgins) had already demonstrated that he could make such a record and from it repeat accurately the precise sounds of the Flower Girl's utterances. Obviously he must have used some type of writing that had more than the five vowel letters of the Roman alphabet. He was using a *phonetic alphabet* and making a *phonetic transcription.*[27]

Because of the insufficient number of letters (especially the lack of letters to represent more than five vowel sounds) scholars who have tried to write about pronunciation matters and to identify the many differences that occur in the speech sounds people use have devised phonetic alphabets. In English the invention and use of special phonetic alphabets goes back at least as far as the work of John Hart, who in 1570 published and used such an alphabet in the teaching of reading. He had already used the "newe maner of writing" in his *Orthographie* of 1569 and discussed it in his manuscript *The Opening of the Unreasonable Writing of Our English Toung* in 1551.

For even so I have opened the vices and faultes of our writing: which cause it to be tedious, and long in learnyng: and learned hard, and evill to read. . . . And then have I sought the meanes (herin writen) by the which we may use a certaine, good and easi writing, onli folowing our pronunciation; and keping the letters in their auncient, Simple, and Singular powers. . . .[28]

Others, like Sir Thomas Smith, William Bullokar, and Edmund Coote in the sixteenth century, Alexander Gill, Charls Butler, and John Wilkins in the seventeenth century, and Benjamin Franklin in the eighteenth century advocated and used phonetic alphabets for English. A. J. Ellis and Isaac Pitman struggled with their Phonotype through the middle of the nineteenth century. But it was the International Phonetic Association (founded in 1886), that took up Otto Jespersen's suggestion and established in 1888 an alphabet designed to be really international and applicable to all languages.[29] In general it was derived from Henry Sweet's Broad and Narrow Romic rather than from Alexander Melville Bell's Visible Speech or Otto Jespersen's Analphabetic System.

The International Phonetic Alphabet (IPA) with additions and improvements has been used ever since 1888 in the *Maître Phonétique,* the official publication of the International Phonetic Association. The chart shows this alphabet as published in 1912. At that time it had symbols for twenty-six different vowel sounds and fifty-two different consonant sounds.

		Lips	Lip-teeth	Point and Blade	Front	Back	Uvula	Throat
CONSONANTS	Plosive	p b		t d	c ɟ	k g	q ɢ	?
	Nasal	m		n	ɲ	ŋ	N	
	Lateral			l ɬ	ʎ	(ɬ)		
	Rolled			r ř			R	
	Fricative	ꜰ ʋ ʍ w ɥ σ ρ	f v	θ ð s z σ ρ ʃ ʒ ɹ	ç j (ɥ)	(ʍ w) x ɣ	ʁ ʀ	h ɦ
VOWELS	Close	(u ü y) (ʊ ʏ)			*Front* i y ɪ ʏ	*Mixed* ï ü	*Back* ɯ u ʊ	
	Half-close	(o ö ø)			e ø	ë ö ə	v o	
	Half-open	(ɔ ɞ̃ œ)			ɛ œ	ɛ̃ ɔ̃ ɐ	ʌ ɔ	
	Open					æ ɐ a ɑ		

(Sounds appearing twice on the chart have a double articulation, the secondary articulation being shown by the symbol in brackets.)
From the Supplement to the Maître Phonétique'Sept.-Oct.1912, entitled, <u>The Principles of the International Phonetic Association.</u> Page 10.

SOURCE: Supplement to the *Maître Phonétique,* September-October 1912, entitled *The Principles of the International Phonetic Association,* p. 10.

But *phonetic transcription,* the use of a phonetic alphabet, is but one of the tools of phonetics, the science of speech sounds. Frequently, however, among those who are actively using phonetic transcriptions in their study of a foreign language, the term *phonetics* has become the equivalent of phonetic transcription. Among those who discuss the problems of teaching reading, *phonetics* and *phonics* have become equivalent terms. Among linguists, *phonetics* is a science devoted to the study of speech sounds. Phonetics in this

(left margin: THE INTERNATIONAL PHONETIC ALPHABET)

sense made great progress during the years 1875–1925, especially in the acoustic analysis of speed sounds.

Just as the "sounds" of languages in their relationships formed the basic materials of the first break-through of modern linguistic science, and constituted the special features of the investigations that led to the second break-through of the 1870s, so it was a new view of the "sounds" as units in a structural system that will appear to lead the way into the linguistic developments from 1925 to 1950.

By 1925, the end of the second fifty years of the modern scientific study of language, the following views of language, of special significance for us, had become for linguists common ground upon which to base their study.[30]

(1) The sound-features of a language (the pronunciation) even of unwritten languages or of the language of the illiterate and uneducated are its most stable characteristic. Sound-changes operate as massive, uniform, and gradual alterations within a particular language or dialect, and within a particular period of time. Sound-changes are neither hindered nor helped by features of meaning, nor by the conscious choices of individuals. The regularity of these sound-changes has made it possible to predict the precise forms of words in a dialect, before actual instances of them have been found.

(2) It became clear, from the fifty years of editorial work upon the *Oxford English Dictionary* and the other collections of usage, that multiple meanings for words is normal, not "queer." We must everywhere in language expect to find that the frequently used words have a variety of meanings—not just one so-called literal meaning and a few figurative or transferred meanings. The number of different meanings for each of the commonly used words of English as recorded and illustrated in the *Oxford English Dictionary* will not be believed without a thorough study of the evidence. For example, for the 500 most used words in English (as listed by the Thorndike word-count) the *Oxford Dictionary* records 14,070 separate and different meanings—an average of 28 different meanings for each word.

(3) The development of the work in phonetics provided the techniques for the successful analysis and description of speech sounds. Now we know that all the "mysterious" qualities of the sounds and "accents" in human languages are matters that can be

analyzed and described in terms of the physical movements by which they are produced, and also in terms of the specific kinds of vibrations that make up their acoustic characteristics. The increasing accuracy and completeness of the recording, reproduction, and transmission of vocal sounds grew out of the work of the phonetics laboratories.

(4) The continued work on the historical dictionaries, and the new work on the surveys of dialect areas which constituted the development of linguistic geography, produced greater understanding not only of the necessity of gathering the facts of usage upon as broad a base as possible but also of the need for more and more rigorous techniques both for collecting these facts and for studying them in order to have them yield sound and significant results.

Usage materials which are mere chance observations, or even usage materials more consistently collected but without the necessary information of all the historical, geographical, and class circumstances in which they occurred, or usage materials without collections of the alternate forms with which they must be compared, or usage materials that provide no basis for quantitative evaluation—such usage materials cannot provide the basis for scientific linguistic study. And even usage materials that provide all the necessary kinds of information in an adequate sampling must be handled rigorously with the accepted appropriate techniques of linguistic analysis.

Just as in 1867 and 1875 William Dwight Whitney's two books attempted to summarize and interpret the new linguistic understanding achieved during the first fifty years of the "new linguistic science," so the second fifty years of that science had its contemporary authors who, in spite of the immensely more complex achievements of the years from 1875 to 1925, tried to bring the summary and interpretation of the new linguistic knowledge up to date:

(1) Hermann Paul, *Prinzipien der Sprachgeschichte,* first edition 1880, fifth edition 1920. The second edition (1886) was translated in 1889 into English by H. A. Strong, entitled *Principles of the History of Language*. An adaptation for English readers was produced by H. A. Strong, W. S. Longman, and B. L. Wheeler, entitled *Introduction to the Study of the History of Languages*.

(2) Leonard Bloomfield, *An Introduction to the Study of Language,* 1914.

(3) Otto Jespersen, *Language, Its Nature, Development, and Origin,* 1921.

(4) Holger Pedersen, *Linguistic Science in the Nineteenth Century,* 1924, translated by John Webster Spargo, 1931.

(5) Edward Sapir, *Language,* 1921.

(6) Leonard Bloomfield, "On Recent Work in General Linguistics," in *Modern Philology* XXV (1927), 211–230.

The last two items of this list not only help to sum up the achievements to 1925 but also lead the way into the new materials of the next thirty-five years.

LINGUISTIC SCIENCE FROM 1925 TO 1950

In general the scientific study of language as practiced in the United States throughout the nineteenth century and during the first quarter of the twentieth century was based upon and did not depart greatly from that of the long line of European scholars working in historical-comparative linguistics, in phonetics, and in linguistic geography. With the breaking of contacts during the two world wars and the difficulty of intimate communication and the interruption of the flow of journals and books during at least ten of the years between the two wars, linguistics or the scientific study of language in the United States has had a somewhat independent but more or less parallel development with that of Europe. Here we shall center attention upon the American developments without special comment upon points of similarity or difference in the European approach.[31]

In America the development of "descriptive" linguistics (*synchronic* rather than *diachronic* description) grew out of the efforts to record and analyze the enormous number of individual languages that were members of the more than fifty separate families of American Indian languages on the North American continent.[32] In Europe, in a quite different way, Ferdinand de Saussure contributed greatly to the broadening of the field of scientific linguistics to include "descriptive" study. De Saussure's contribution did not come from any large amount of detailed descriptive analyses of living languages. It was rather a discussion and demonstration of fundamental linguistic principles. Bloomfield, in reviewing the second edition (1922) of de Saussure's book (composed primarily from notes taken by his students) praised it in enthusiastic terms, "The essential point . . . is this, that de Saussure has here first mapped out the world in which historical Indo-European grammar (the great achievement of the past century) is merely a single province; he has given us the theoretic basis for a science of human speech."[33]

Edward Sapir contributed tremendously to the newer trend which made "descriptive" language study acceptably scientific. The influence of his *Language,* 1921, is still strong. Leonard Bloomfield, in his review of that book in 1922, welcomed it as part of the changing emphasis in linguistics: "We are coming to believe that restriction to historical work is unreasonable and, in the long run methodically impossible. One is glad to see, that Dr. Sapir deals with synchronic matters (to use de Saussure's terminology) before he deals with diachronic, and gives to the former as much space as to the latter."[34]

The Break-through of American "Structural Linguistics"

For American "structural linguistics" that has given special vigor to the linguistic work in this country since 1925, Edward Sapir furnished the basic point of view and Leonard Bloomfield provided the detailed statement of principles of analysis. To mark the beginning then of the third, the present period of linguistic science in the United States, we would point to the publishing of Edward Sapir's "Sound Patterns in Language" in the first volume of the official journal of the Linguistic Society of America, *Language* (1925). This article represents, I believe, the break-through into the new approach which has developed into our "structural linguistics." Indeed, the present period of the scientific study of language has become the period of "structural linguistics."[35] But Sapir's paper of 1925 was not his first statement of the new point of view. In his book *Language* (1921), in the latter part of Chapter III, "The Sounds of Language," he had already expressed the beginnings from which his "structuralism" grew. Back of it lay his experience with his informant when he was trying to record, analyze, and describe some of the languages of the Athabaskan family of American Indian languages.

> I found that it was difficult or impossible to teach an Indian to make phonetic distinctions that did not correspond to "points in the pattern of his language," however these differences might strike our objective ear, but that subtle, barely audible phonetic differences, if only they hit the "points in the pattern," were easily and voluntarily expressed in writing. . . .
>
> Two historically related languages or dialects may not have a sound in common, but their ideal sound-systems may be identical patterns.[36]

Sapir's article of 1925 is a fully developed demonstration with the evidence of both the negative and the positive aspects of his general statement.

> It is very necessary to understand that it is not because the objective difference is too slight to be readily perceptible that such variations as the quantitative alternations in *bad* and *bat, bead* and *beat, fade* and *fate* stand outside of the proper phonetic pattern of the language (e.g., are not psychologically parallel to such qualitative-quantitative alternations as *bid* and *bead, fed* and *fade,* or to such quantitative alternations as German *Schlaf* and *schlaff,* Latin *āra* and *ārā*), but that the objective difference is felt to be slight precisely because it corresponds to nothing significant in the inner structure of the phonetic pattern. In matters of this kind, objective estimates of similarity or difference, based either on specific linguistic habits or on a generalized phonetic system, are utterly fallacious. As a matter of fact, the mechanical English vocalic relation *bad : bat* would in many languages be quite marked enough to indicate a relation of distinct points of the pattern, while the English pattern relation -t : -d, which seems so self-evidently real to us, has in not a few other languages either no reality at all or only a mechanical, conditional one.

> After what we have said, it almost goes without saying that two languages, A and B, may have identical sounds but utterly distinct phonetic patterns; or they may have mutually incompatible phonetic systems, from the articulatory and acoustic standpoint, but identical or similar patterns.

> Phonetic patterning helps also to explain why people find it difficult to pronounce certain foreign sounds which they possess in their own language. Thus, a Nootka Indian in pronouncing English words with ŋ or *l* invariably substitutes *n* for each of these sounds. Yet he is able to pronounce both ŋ and *l*. He does not use these sounds in prose dis-

course, but ŋ is very common in the chants and *l* is often substituted for *n* in songs. His feeling for the stylistic character of ŋ and for the *n-l* equivalence prevents him from "hearing" English ŋ and *l* correctly. Here again we see that a speech sound is not merely an articulation or an acoustic image, but material for symbolic expression in an appropriate linguistic context.[37]

Two facts, especially important for us here, came out of Sapir's experience.

(a) The same phonetic difference may have (and probably will have) entirely different structural values from language to language.

(b) There is power or force in the structural system itself. The habits that constitute the control of one's native language are not habits concerning items as items, but habits concerning contrastive items as functioning units of an *ordered system of structural patterns.*

In 1926 Leonard Bloomfield published his "Postulates for the Study of Language."[38] In 1927 appeared his article "On Recent Work in General Linguistics."[39] But the most important single publication concerning the scientific study of language during the last thirty-five years was Bloomfield's book, *Language* (1933). Professor Bernard Bloch, of Yale, writing the following sentences in 1949, does not overstate the situation.

It is not too much to say that every significant refinement of analytic method produced in this country since 1930 has come as a direct result of the impetus given to linguistic research by Bloomfield's book. If today our methods are in some ways better than his, if we see more clearly than he did himself certain aspects of structure that he first revealed to us, it is because we stand upon his shoulders.[40]

Bloomfield considered his book of 1933 a revision of his *Introduction to the Study of Language* of 1914, of which he said:

Its purpose is the same . . . as that of Whitney's *Language and the Study of Language* and *The Life and Growth of Language,* books which fifty years ago represented the attainments of linguistic science, and, owing to their author's clearness of view and conscious discrimination between ascertained fact and mere surmise, contain little to which we cannot today subscribe.[41]

Bloomfield's *Language,* 1933, therefore, was an effort again to bring to the educated public the new knowledge and understanding of human language that had been achieved up to the time of writing. It is especially noteworthy that this book that presents a large part of the substance of the linguistic achievement of the period beginning in 1925 was published in 1933 when the new work had hardly got under way. In contrast, Whitney's books of 1867 and 1875 came at the end of a period of fifty years, as did those that gathered the new knowledge for the second fifty years. Bloomfield's book led the way into the achievements of present-day American "structural linguistics."

The present wide use of the term *structural linguistics* does not mean that all practicing linguists today agree upon what constitutes the special identifying features of this structuralism. The evidence for this great diversity of view shows itself in the articles listed by Kenneth and Eunice Pike in their bibliography covering the *Live Issues in Descriptive Linguistics* (1960) and in the references with critical comments that appear in the three parts of Kenneth Pike's *Language in Relation to a Unified Theory of the Structure of Human Behavior* (1954, 1955, 1960).

Rather than attempt to show the strands of this variety I shall here try simply to give a brief statement of some of the views of language and the principles of practice of a structural approach that stems primarily from the writings of Edward Sapir and Leonard Bloomfield.[42]

Structural Units and Word-Patterns

Our "structural" approach requires a basic shift in the usual thinking about language. For most people, that thinking is *word-centered*. As a child develops during his first and second years, we try to count the "words that he knows" as the measure of his progress in learning to talk. In the schools, the practical considerations of language problems have almost completely dealt with the words. Books are examined and rated on the basis of the kind and number of the words used. Readability scales and measures of grade placement for reading materials give primary attention to vocabulary items. Many of the discussions of the teaching of reading center upon the problems of word recognition and the learning of "new" words. Foreign language study usually features the number and range of the words mastered. Everywhere there is the pressure for increasing the size of one's vocabulary. Words and their meanings have held the central place in our thinking about language for so long a time that it has become extremely difficult for many people to realize even the existence of the kind of *structural base that constitutes the essential feature of every part of language.* It will probably be a long time before all who teach the language arts appreciate fully the significance of Sapir's comment of more than forty years ago: "The linguistic student should never make the mistake of identifying a language with its dictionary."[43]

This structuralism not only requires us to abandon our word-centered thinking about language; it demands that in every aspect of language we must shift from an *item-centered* view to one that is *structure-centered.* Language learning, in the thinking of both laymen and teachers, most frequently has meant the mastering of *items*—the items of sound that must be pronounced, the individual words that must be identified with meanings, the parts of sentences that must be classified.

From our structural point of view, items such as these have no linguistic significance by themselves. Only as such items contrast with other items in the patterns of an arbitrary system do they have linguistic significance. In other words, all the significant matters of language are linguistic features in contrast. Of course any difference between two items can be said to establish a basis upon which to assert that the two items are in contrast. But for the purposes of language—that is, language as a code of signals to transmit meanings[44]—not every possible physical contrast that makes two items different is used by every language or any particular language. We are concerned here with the special linguistic contrasts that English uses as the functioning units to identify and distinguish the patterns that constitute its structure.

For example, in English, as in other languages, of the many differences between vocal sounds that occur, only a very limited number are used as the units that function to identify lexical items or "words." English uses the difference between sounds made by the stopping of the breath in the mouth by the tip of the tongue against the alveolar ridge (the gums) and the sound made by stopping it by the base of the tongue against the palate (the roof of the mouth). This is the contrastive difference of sound between /tɪn/ *tin* and

/kɪn/ *kin,* /tæn/ *tan* and /kæn/ *can,* /ton/ *tone* and /kon/ *cone,*
/pɪt/ *pit* and /pɪk/ *pick,* /pæt/ *pat* and /pæk/ *pack,* /nat/ *knot*
and /nak/ *knock.*[45] This contrastive difference between /t/ and
/k/ as used in English to identify and distinguish a large number
of word patterns makes /t/ and /k/ two of the functioning units
of the structure of our sound system—of our pronunciation.

But the particular sounds represented by *p* in *pin, pan, pun*
differ phonetically from those represented by *p* in *spin, span, spun.*
The initial consonant of *pin, pan, pun* is followed by a strong puff
of breath, an aspiration, which does not occur after the same consonant in *spin, span, spun.* This difference between the aspirated
consonant sound and the unaspirated consonant sound, however, is
never used in English to distinguish word patterns. Therefore the
aspirated consonant sound [pʰ] is not a separate functioning unit
of our pronunciation structure.

In similar fashion, the initial /k/ in each of the following
words /kɪl/ *kill,* /kol/ *coal,* /kɔl/ *call* differs phonetically from the
other two. The initial consonant sound in *kill* is made by the base
of the tongue touching the roof of the mouth farther forward than
it does in making the initial consonant sound in *coal,* and much
farther forward than in making the initial consonant sound in *call.*
But these phonetic differences do not make these three different
sounds separate functioning units of our pronunciation structure.
These three instances of /k/ (the /k/ in *kill,* the /k/ in *coal,* the
/k/ in *call*), differ phonetically, but English does not use these
particular phonetic differences to identify and distinguish word
patterns. They constitute a single functioning or signaling unit of
our word patterns—a *phoneme.*

"Structural" linguistics has attempted to discover and to describe the contrastive sound units (the bundles of contrastive sound
features) that function in each language to identify and separate
the various lexical units (morphemes or "words"). To this end it
has developed sets of special techniques. For example, to determine
for English the number and kind of vowel sounds that are structurally significant (the vowel structural units of English) one can
seek quite simply the words differentiated solely by different vowels.
He will not find, as functioning units in the sound patterns that
identify words, the 130 different vowel sounds that Higgins could
hear, nor even the 24 that Pickering could distinguish. In each of

the following sets of words the sounds of the consonant frames in which the vowel appears are the same: /p—l/ and /h—t/. The vowel sounds alone (we must ignore the conventional spellings) make the difference.

> *peal,* /pil/; *pell,* /pɛl/   (as in pell-mell); *pool,* /pul/;
> *pill,* /pɪl/; *pal,* /pæl/;   *pull,* /pʊl/;
> *pale,* /pel/; *poll,* /pal/ (as in poll parrot); *pole,* /pol/;
>   *Paul,* /pɔl/.

But we do not have in English a word of this consonant frame /p—l/ with the vowel unit /ə/, as in the words *hut, but, cut.* In the series with the consonant pattern /h—t/, however, this vowel /ə/ appears as a distinguishing feature, as in *hut* /hət/. The /h—t/ series uses the following contrastive vowels in addition to the /ə/ in *hut:*

> *heat,* /hit/;   *hat,* /hæt/;
> *hit,* /hɪt/;   *hot,* /hat/;
> *hate,* /het/;   *hoot,* /hut/.
> *het,* /hɛt/ (in "nonstandard" English)

There is no /hʊt/ to rhyme with *foot,* and no /hot/ to rhyme with *boat.*

Of vowel clusters or diphthongs there are in English *file,* /faɪl/ (/a + ɪ/), *fowl,* /faʊl/ (/a + ʊ/), and *foil* /fɔɪl/ (/ɔ + ɪ/).

From this structural point of view, English uses, as contrastive units to identify and distinguish words, eleven single vowels and three vowel clusters. There are in English speech a tremendous number of different vowel sounds that can be heard, isolated, and described, but I can find in my speech only these eleven vowel units or bundles of phonetic features that contrast with each other to form the functioning units of the sound patterns that identify words. Structural linguistics thus seeks to identify the contrastive units that function in some particular language like English to distinguish or separate the various word patterns.

Structural linguistics also seeks to discover the particular sequences in which these units occur within the word-patterns, for, in the languages that have been described, it appears that the permitted sequences differ for each language and are strictly limited. In English, for example, the last consonant of the word *king* /kɪŋ/ - /ŋ/ - never occurs initially in a word. It always comes after a vowel. In English, there are at least 100 different consonant clusters that occur at the ends of words, as /nd/ in *sand, bend, wind;* /lt/ in *wilt, built, bolt;* /gd/ in *tagged, wagged, sagged;* /lθ/ in *health, wealth, stealth;* /kt/ in *walked, talked, looked;* /lz/ in *calls, holes, peals.* And there are at least 40 other consonant clusters that occur at the beginnings of words, as /gl/ in *glad, glisten, gloom;* /br/ in *bread, broom, brick;* /sn/ in *sneeze, snare, snow;* /tw/ in *twist, twine, tweezers.* But of all these clusters, *only three*—/st/, /sp/, /sk/—*occur both at the beginnings and at the ends of words* —*stain, rust; spell, lisp; skin, mask.* Many possible clusters of consonants do not occur at all either initially or finally in English, /dm/ (except internally with syllable division as in *Skidmore* College); /mk/ (except internally with syllable division as in the compound *tram-car*), /šn/ (except by those who show signs of intoxication).

With these developments in structural analysis it has become clear that practical pronunciation problems are for the most part not matters of the phonetic character of the sound segments *per se,* but rather, matters of the units and the *patterns of the structure* of the pronunciation system. The habits of pronunciation that the child develops in learning his native language are not habits of producing and hearing the separate sounds as isolatable items in individual words but rather habits of patterns of functioning contrasts in the unique structured system of a particular language.

The child learns to hear and to pronounce with speed and precision the contrastive features of the units in the sequences used to identify and separate the word patterns. But his speed and precision are achieved also, in part, by learning to *ignore* the phonetic features that are not structurally significant for his particular language. Thus the automatic habits through which we manipulate our native language signals have also developed blind spots for contrastive language features outside the structural system of our own particular language. We would now measure the child's first progress in learning to talk, not by counting the number of "words" he is said to "know," but by the degree to which he has achieved the production of, and responses to, the functioning contrasts by which *words* (and the other types of language signals) are identified.

To "know" a word means, in the first place, the instant recognition, in the stream of speech, of the particular pattern of functioning contrasts that identifies that word. To "know" a word means also, in the second place, a similarly instant recognition of some bundle of experience with which the word pattern is associated. The bundle of experience thus brought into attention with a word pattern in an utterance constitutes its "meaning." A child "learns" the physical word patterns /fađər/ *father* and /məđər/ *mother* only once; but as he matures he keeps constantly changing and enlarging the content of the bundle of experience which he correlates with these word patterns, until it comprehends an adult understanding of male and female parenthood. In respect to words, then, a child's competence at any particular age consists of the physical word patterns he recognizes *and* the bundles of experience with which the word patterns correlate for him. Practice in the use of the language makes the recognition and the correlation extremely rapid, until the signaling physical pattern itself sinks completely below the threshold of attention, leaving only the bundles of experience or the meaning of the utterance as a whole.

Structural Units and Grammar

Our structural linguistics does not confine itself to the bundles of contrastive sound features that in special sequences identify the word patterns of our language. The identification of the word patterns constitutes only the beginnings of the efforts of the structuralist to discover the chief features of the nature of language and the processes by which it accomplishes its communicative purposes. "Knowing" at least some of the thousands of words that a language uses constitutes only one of the essentials of communication.

As indicated above, words have held the central place in the layman's thinking about language. Examples of this word-centered thinking are abundant. During the past six years I have found views practically identical with those expressed in the following quotation vigorously put forward and argued by language teachers in countries as far apart as Germany and Japan.

In English, words are formed into sentences by the operation of an invisible power, which is like magnetism. Each one is charged with a meaning which gives it a tendency toward some of those in the sentence, and particularly to one, and which repels it from others; and he who subtly divines and dexterously uses this attraction, filling his words with a living but latent light and heat, which makes them leap to each other and cling together while they transmit his freely-flowing thought, is a master of the English language, although he may be ignorant and uninstructed in its use.[46]

Present-day examples of the continuation of word-centered thinking concerning sentences are abundant. In the UNESCO monograph on *The Teaching of Reading and Writing* (1956), Professor W. S. Gray, of the University of Chicago, writes of what he calls "fusing the meanings of words into ideas." He gives the following sentence and then attempts to account for the meaning it conveys.

> *The water in our village well is good to drink.*

As one reads the first two words in this sentence various associations are aroused. This grasp of meanings is restricted and made more definite as the third, fourth, fifth and sixth words are recognized. The thoughts then retained are held in mind, as the reader continues to the end of the sentence. When he recognizes the words, "good to drink," the meaning already acquired is greatly expanded and clarified. The final idea is the result of the fusion of the meanings of the separate words into a coherent whole.[47]

As it stands, this sentence, "The water in our village well is good to drink," is a report or statement of the fact that the water is drinkable. But the simple shifting of the word *is* to the beginning, as in "Is the water in our village well good to drink," makes the "final idea" from these same words a question rather than the report or statement of a fact. To use these identical words in other positions would give us entirely different "final ideas."

> To drink the well water in our village is good.
>
> To water well the drink in our village is good.

Even the very different meanings to be attached to the same word-pattern, *well,* are indicated by the contrasting structural sets in which the word appears—*the well water, to water well.*

From the structural point of view adopted here, the "final idea" of this sentence as a whole—"The water in our village well is good to drink"—does *not* result from "the fusion of the meanings of the separate words into a meaningful whole." The full linguistic meaning of this sentence cannot be derived from a fusion of any or all of the meanings of these ten separate words—even with the amazing number of different meanings recorded for each of them in the *Oxford Dictionary*. There is a layer of meanings apart from those of the words as separate lexical items. These meanings can be called *grammatical meanings*.

Grammatical meanings are not merely vague inferences from the context—whether of the words used or of the features of the practical situation in which an utterance occurs. They are definite and sharp, essential features of every utterance; and, like the bundles of experience arbitrarily attached to physical word-patterns, also arbitrarily attached to specific patterns of contrastive features of arrangement and form. Since the connections of these "meanings" with the patterns of contrastive arrangement and form are arbitrary they must be definitely learned. As in the case of the physical word-patterns and their meanings, also with long practice and use, the recognition responses to the specific patterns of contrastive arrangement and form sink below the threshold of attention and leave only the grammatical meanings that are signaled.

In the matter of word-patterns and their meanings, the learning continues throughout life and we remember many of the instances of vocabulary learning. For grammatical meanings and the patterns of arrangement and form with which they are tied, the learning for each of us in our native language took place so early that we do not remember any of that learning, nor even that there is anything on this level that had to be learned.

The traditional grammar that has been taught in our schools for more than 150 years has simply assumed that the meanings here called grammatical meanings are intuitive and has never raised the question as to the means by which they are identified. For example, given the sentence,

> Employers usually pay their workers good wages.

the traditional grammar calls attention to some of the meanings it communicates, and assigns names to those meanings.

(a) This sentence makes a *statement* or a *report* of a fact. It does not ask a question nor does it make a request or give a command. This sentence is therefore assigned the technical name *declarative sentence.* A question sentence would be assigned the technical name *interrogative sentence,* and a request or command sentence given the technical name *imperative sentence.*

(b) The given sentence identifies the *performers of the action* as *employers.* This word *employers* is therefore assigned the technical name *subject.* The *action performed* is identified as that of *paying.* Therefore the word *pays* is assigned the technical name *predicate* (*verb*). The *thing paid* is identified as *wages;* therefore the word *wages* is assigned the technical name *direct object.* And so on through the whole sentence.

In other words the traditional grammar starts from the meanings, which are assumed to be intuitive responses to the whole string of words as lexical items, and requires that the particular words and the groups of words to which these meanings are applied be assigned certain technical names. The whole process seems to be one of an analysis of the meanings for the sake of assigning certain technical names to particular words and word groups.

Our structural approach to grammar differs fundamentally in purpose and assumptions from that of the traditional school grammar. It recognizes all the grammatical *meanings* of the traditional grammar but does not accept either of the assumptions—(a) that the recognition of these meanings are intuitive responses, or (b) that they arise out of the fusion of the meanings of the separate words. This structural approach assumes that whatever "grammatical meanings" there are, are definitely conveyed by signals; that these signals consist of structures, identified by contrastive patterns of functioning structural "units"; and that these patterns can be described in terms of the contrastive arrangements and forms of these functioning "units."

Classification as such does not constitute any part of the goal of the structural linguistics here presented. Our structural approach seeks to identify and describe the *contrastive patterns of form and arrangement* which *regularly elicit predictable responses in a particular linguistic community.*[48] As in the case of the patterns of sound that identify the lexical items or "words," the structural approach to grammar differentiates sharply between those items that are functioning contrasts in the identifying of grammatical signals and those features of form and arrangement which do not so function. In grammar, too, the number of units that, in any particular language, function in regularly eliciting predictable responses is only a strictly limited part of those that exist.

For example, in all languages, the "words" of the utterances must occur in some order—in some sequence in a time dimension. But in only a limited number of languages does a contrast of position in the utterance sequences signal any grammatical meanings. In Old English the meaning of "performer of the action" in *"þone beran slōh sē mann"* is signalled by a structure identified solely by the contrastive forms of the article, *sē,* the nominative form, as attached to *mann* in contrast with *þone,* the accusative form, as attached to *beran.* The actual position of these words in the time sequence, *þone beran* as preceding *slōh* (the verb) in contrast with *sē mann* as following *slōh,* has no grammatical signalling value in distinguishing the "performer" of the action of "killing" from the "undergoer." These words *þone beran* and *sē mann* could occur in any position of the sequence (*sē mann þone beran slōh,* or *þone beran sē mann slōh,* or *sē mann slōh þone beran*) and we could predict that the regular response of any native speaker of Old English would be a recognition of the fact that the man (*sē mann*) performed the act of killing and that it was the bear (*þone beran*) that did not survive. In Modern English, however, with no contrasting forms of the article, the sentence "The man killed the bear" is just as definite and precise in eliciting the recognition response that *the man* performed the action and *the bear* did not survive. In Modern English it is the contrastive position of *the man* and *the bear* in the sequence that constitutes the structure that signals the meaning identifying the "performer" and the "undergoer." A shift in the position in the sequence to "The bear killed the man" would elicit a very different response—the recognition now of *the bear* as "the performer" and *the man* as "undergoer." The sequence "The man the bear killed" would elicit no predictable response as to which was the performer and which the undergoer.

The structuralist assumes that the habits that constitute the control of one's own native language are not habits concerning items of language as separate items—that is, of separate segments of sound as represented by the separate letters of an alphabet, or of individual grammatical forms. He assumes rather that practical language habits are always habits concerning contrastive forms and arrangements of linguistic items, in patterns of structure functioning as signals in a system. He attempts to discover and to describe

(a) the basic contrastive bundles of sound features that constitute the units that identify and separate the lexical items;

(b) the basic contrastive markers that identify and separate the units that constitute the patterns of grammatical structure;

(c) the basic contrastive arrangements of the patterns of grammatical structure that regularly elicit recognition responses of grammatical or structural meanings.

We cannot predict whether a certain person will speak at a given moment, or what he will say, or in what words and other linguistic forms he will say it. These are acts of *speech* (*la parole*). The sum of the speech acts of a community, however, does not constitute its *language*. The *language* (*la langue*) is the rigid system of patterns of contrastive features through which the individual speech acts of a speaker become effective substitute stimuli (signals) for a hearer. With this rigid system of patterns *we can predict* the patterns of the regular responses of the members of a linguistic community, when they are effectively stimulated by one of the patterns of the system. Descriptive structural analysis has as its goal such a descriptive statement of the patterns of a language system that we may "calculate" these regular patterns of responses to the patterned signals.

The field of linguistic science has been greatly enriched by the modern emphases upon "descriptive" linguistics. "Historical" linguistics has not been superseded by "description." The basic understanding of "structure" which developed at first primarily within the struggle to describe a great many widely diverse living languages is equally significant for both synchronic and for diachronic study.[49] The field of modern linguistic science has broadened greatly but it has been considerably unified by increasing "structural" insights.

For other materials that have surveyed the developments in linguistics from 1925 to 1950 see the following items:

(1) Robert A. Hall, "American Linguistics 1925–1950," *Archivum Linguisticum,* III (1951), 101–125, and IV (1952), 1–16.

(2) George S. Lane, "Changes of Emphasis in Linguistics with Particular Reference to Paul and Bloomfield," *Studies in Philology* XLII (1945), 465–483. See also *Studies in Philology* XLIII (1946), 461–464, for "Comment" by George L. Trager.

Throughout this chapter, attention has centered upon the growing understanding of certain features of the nature and functioning of human language, which has been achieved by the devoted labors of a host of linguistic scholars during the last 140 years. Primary attention has centered upon the results—especially the unexpected results—of these labors rather than upon the developing rigor with which new techniques, new tools, and new procedures have been employed. Some linguists have at times given the impression that, for them, the new techniques, procedures, and classificatory definitions alone constituted the substance of linguistic science. I do not want to belittle the scientific importance of sound techniques, rigorous procedures, and sharp classifications. I should like, however, to insist that one can achieve a sufficient mastery of the tools, techniques, and procedures of linguistic analysis to be a good practitioner in analyzing and describing languages, without any real understanding of the important achievements which constitute the substance of linguistic science.

SUMMARIES

In each of the three periods in the development of modern linguistic science several important characteristics of human language have become clear and have become part of the assumptions upon which later linguistic work was built.

By 1875, the end of the first fifty years, the following views of language had become acceptable assumptions upon which to base procedures.

(1) Constant change is to be expected in all languages at every period of their history.

(2) These changes are not a succession of unrelated events in which anything can happen at random. In spite of what seemed to be many exceptions, they showed so much regularity that it was possible to grasp the correspondences of form in generalizations

upon which to determine language relationship and establish "families" of languages. The assumption of a basic regularity of change made possible scientific investigation.

(3) The changes of language could not have been the result of corruptions arising out of the mistakes of ignorant and careless speakers. Only by assuming that the regular usage of the speakers and writers of a language (community) furnish the only basis of correctness for that language (community) could such a dictionary as the *Oxford English Dictionary* have been conceived and produced.

By 1925, the end of the second fifty years, the following views of language had become for linguists common assumptions upon which to base their studies.

(1) The sound features of a language, even of unwritten languages, or of the language of the illiterate and uneducated, are its most stable features. Sound-changes operate in massive, uniform, and gradual alterations within a particular language or dialect, and within a particular period of time. Sound-changes are neither hindered nor helped by features of meaning, nor by the conscious choices of individuals. The regularity of these sound changes has made it possible to predict the precise forms of words in a dialect, or related language, before actual instances of them have been found.

(2) Multiple meanings for words is normal, not "queer." We must everywhere expect in language to find that the frequently used words have a surprising variety of meanings—not just one so-called literal meaning and a few figurative or transferred meanings.

(3) All the "mysterious" qualities of the sounds and "accents" of languages (and dialects) can be analyzed and described in terms of the physical movements by which they are produced, and also in terms of the specific kinds of vibrations that make up their acoustic characteristics.

(4) With the acceptance of the general assumption that the regular usage of the native speakers of a language constitutes the only basis for "correctness," as the basic principle upon which to carry out the work on historical dictionaries and the surveys of dialect areas which produced linguistic geography, there also

developed a greater understanding of the varieties of usage and the necessity for more and more rigorous controls, both in collecting the facts and in studying them. In order to have usage materials yield sound and significant results, these materials must not be mere chance observations. To provide the basis for any sound linguistic study, they must be consistently and systematically collected through an adequately controlled sampling process, and provide all the essential information of the historical, geographical, and social class circumstances in which the utterances occurred. They must contain the alternate forms with which they need to be compared and enough examples to make a quantitative evaluation significant. But even usage materials that provide all these necessary kinds of information in an adequate sampling, to be useful, must be handled rigorously with appropriate established techniques for linguistic analysis.

The years since 1925, the third period in the development of linguistic science, have again provided new insights into the nature and functioning of language—a basic reorientation which not only makes fruitful a restudy of the data formerly collected for descriptive and historical work, but also, when patiently explored, sheds new light on all the problems of communication and understanding.

Some of the new views which have resulted from or stimulated the linguistic activity of the past thirty-five years are the following.

(1) Language is structured. This structuring is a basic characteristic of every aspect of human language and has made it capable of more than the simple calls and commands. It has given human language the power to grasp and to communicate highly complicated reports. The languages of even the most "primitive" peoples have this basic structural characteristic, and are also capable of grasping and communicating similarly complicated reports. Such reports have made human language the storehouse of man's experience, built up and passed on from generation to generation. Through language, the knowledge and the wisdom won by the most intelligent and the most courageous individual of a group can become the knowledge and the wisdom of all those to whom he can talk. With language a man is no longer a puny individual learning only what he can from his own limited reactions to nature.

Through language he becomes a "group" man, receiving a tremendous inheritance from the accumulated experiences remembered and reported by those who lived before him.

(2) The basic material out of which a language is made consists of audible modifications of the breath-stream—vocal sounds. It has become clear, however, that that which is objectively the same uttered sound will be perceived and responded to very differently by those who speak different languages. In other words, the same phonetic differences usually have entirely different structural values from language to language.

(3) In general, there are no language sounds that are easy or difficult in themselves. Ease or difficulty of hearing or of pronunciation turns out to be a function of the way the phonetic material patterns in a person's native language. Native speakers of English produce and respond easily to the differences between /r/ and /l/ as structural units differentiating word-patterns: *race / lace; ram / lamb; river / liver; correction / collection; gentry / gently; pray / play*. Native Japanese speakers, in the early stages of learning English, find it difficult not only to produce these contrasts systematically; they cannot hear them well enough to differentiate these pairs of words when they are pronounced in immediate sequence, either in isolation or in minimum contrastive sentences. Japanese speakers would find it difficult to determine whether the following three sentences, given orally, are all alike *in meaning,* all different, or two alike and one different.

> They took the long road home.
> They took the wrong road home.
> They took the wrong load home.

(4) The child in learning his native language not only develops great facility and accuracy in responding to the limited number of contrastive units that identify the word-patterns and the grammatical structures of his particular language; he also, in developing this great skill, learns to ignore all those physical features that are not relevant to the identification of these word- and sentence-patterns. He thus, if limited to his native language and dialect, increasingly develops blind spots for a whole range of physical differences that constitute the contrastive, identifying units

of other languages. Thus the power or force in the structural arrangements of the first language (the native language) makes the
learning of a second language as an adult a very different matter
from the learning of the first language. The application of this
principle to other aspects of social behavior, especially as stimulated
by Edward Sapir, has given rise to significant results concerning the
social-cultural meanings of language in relation to the problems of
understanding across linguistic and cultural boundaries.

> The fact of the matter is that the "real world" is to a large extent
> unconsciously built upon the language habits of the group. No two
> languages are ever sufficiently similar to be considered as representing
> the same social reality. The worlds in which different societies live are
> distinct worlds, not merely the same world with different labels at-
> tached.[50]

(5) The units which function in identifying the word-patterns
and the sentence-patterns of a language like English do not consist
of items of vocal sound features added together as building blocks.
These functioning units are bundles of contrastive differences—
contrastive differences of sound features, of sequences, of distribution, of pitch. They are abstractions. Physically, of course, each
speech act consists of a succession of sound waves, of varying
frequency, intensity, length, and so on. Broadly speaking, there
never is or can be an exact repetition of any particular succession
of sound waves as produced and heard. Precise measurements and
accurate recordings always reveal some differences. But in a linguistic community two or more physically different speech acts may
fit into a single functioning pattern and thus may be functionally
the "same." Basically, then, the material that constitutes language
must be recurring "sames" of speech acts. The sum of the speech
acts of a community does not, however, constitute its language.
Only as the sequences of a speech act are grasped or recognized as
fitting into recurring patterns of "sames" of vocal sounds do they
become the stuff out of which language is made. And only when
these patterns of vocal "sames" are correlated with recurring
"sames" of practical situations in man's experience, and thus become the means of eliciting "sames" of predictable responses, do
they become language itself. From this point of view the following
statement might serve as a definition of a *language*.

A language is a system of recurring sequences or patterns of "sames" of vocal sounds which correlate with recurring "sames" of stimulus-situation features, and which elicit recurring "sames" of response features.

A differently phrased definition is given by Sapir in his *Language,* 1921. "Language is a purely human and non-instinctive method of communicating ideas, emotions, and desires, by means of a system of voluntarily produced symbols."[51]

THE LAST TEN YEARS: 1950–1960

No survey of the growing insights into the nature and functioning of human language which have resulted, often unexpectedly, from the professional activities, during the last 140 years, of those devoted to linguistic science should stop short of at least a brief glance at the especially vigorous new linguistic activity of the last ten years.

Applications of Linguistic Knowledge

Of course there had been efforts to apply the developing linguistic knowledge even during the first period of Modern Linguistic Science. Whitney, in 1875, speaks of linguistic science as "bringing about a re-cast of the old methods of teaching even familiar and long-studied languages, like Latin and Greek," and says that it "has leavened all the connected branches of knowledge, and worked itself into the very structure of modern thought."[52] The *Oxford English Dictionary* (first named *A New English Dictionary on Historical Principles; Founded Mainly on the Materials Collected by the Philological Society*) was conceived and carried out as a practical tool for scholars, using in its construction the "methods and results of the new Philological science."

The linguistic science of the nineteenth century, especially the work in phonetics, lay back of the efforts to reform the teaching of languages in Europe, beginning in 1886 with Wilhelm Vietor's *Der Sprachunterricht muss umkehren.* Among the books of this time devoted to applying the results of linguistic science were, in English, Henry Sweet's *Practical Study of Languages: A Guide for Teachers and Learners,* 1900, and Otto Jespersen's *How to Teach a Foreign*

Language, 1903. This revolt from the older and widely used grammar-translation method of teaching language led to what was called "The Direct Method."

Early in the twentieth century also, Professor Thomas R. Lounsbury, of Yale University, attempted to bring to the attention of English teachers and the general reading public the practical significance of some aspects of the developing linguistic knowledge—*English Spelling and Spelling Reform,* 1902, *The Standard of Pronunciation in English,* 1904, and *The Standard of Usage in English,* 1907.

My own book *The Teaching of the English Language* (Thomas Nelson and Sons, 1927) is, as the Preface asserts, "an effort to interpret the modern scientific view of language in a practical way for teachers."[53] It deals with the problems of divided usage in grammar, pronunciation, and vocabulary, as well as those of the developing of language habits, attitudes, and tools, in terms of the knowledge won by linguistic science up to 1925. My *American English Grammar,* 1940, attempted to furnish the materials upon which to build the kind of school grammars indicated by the earlier book as necessary:

> We need a grammar that describes the forms and syntax of present-day American English accurately; a grammar that records the facts of the actual usage of those who are carrying on the affairs of English-speaking people and does not falsify the account in accord with a make-believe standard of "school-mastered" speech; a grammar that explains these facts in the light of their history, not by means of an *a priori* reasoning; and finally, a grammar that attempts to set forth the patterns or tendencies that have shown themselves in the drift of the English language.[54]

A later book, *The Structure of English,*[55] sought to provide some of the basic linguistic materials upon which to build a practical approach to sentence structure.

The specific application of the results of American linguistic science since 1925 to the problems of teaching English as a foreign language began in 1938 with the search for sound materials. *English Word Lists: A Study of Their Adaptability for Instruction*[56] was published in 1940, and Kenneth L. Pike's *Pronunciation,* 1942, contains not only exercises and explanations based upon a phonemic comparison of English and Spanish but also (pp. 25–97) *the results of the first structural study of the intonation of American English.*[57]

Beginning in 1941 the English Language Institute in its research, in its teaching of English as a foreign language, in its production of texts, tests, and other classroom and laboratory materials, and in its teacher training program, has devoted all its resources to the application of the results of modern linguistic science. The basic principles of the approach underlying the work of the English Language Institute are described in a volume entitled *Teaching and Learning English as a Foreign Language.*[58]

Language Learning: A Quarterly Journal of Applied Linguistics has, since beginning publication in January, 1948, served those of many countries who are interested in exploring modern linguistics for help in dealing with the problems of understanding between those of differing linguistic and cultural backgrounds.[59]

A recent book that develops more specifically the applications of linguistic science to the problems of teaching English as a foreign language is entitled *Foundations for English Teaching.*[60] It contains a more detailed discussion of the principles underlying the selection and organization of the English materials of structure and vocabulary, as well as a discussion of the use of dialogue form and the teaching procedures of the oral approach. It contains also a *programmed* set of basic structure-centered English materials with a near-minimum vocabulary in significant lexical sets, as a corpus upon which to base classroom texts and teachers guides.

For the efforts to apply modern linguistic knowledge to the teaching of foreign languages in the United States the article by William G. Moulton of Princeton University, entitled "Linguistics and Language Teaching in the United States 1940–1960"[61] presents the best over-all view.

The most significant application of linguistic knowledge to foreign language learning for the purposes not only of full communication and understanding but also of scientific description and precise and effective translation, has been undertaken and developed by the Summer Institute of Linguistics of the Wycliffe Bible Translators. This organization was founded in 1935 by a man of broad vision, W. Cameron Townsend, who believed that missionaries must thoroughly "understand" the people to whom they go, and to that end must understand and speak the languages of these people much more thoroughly than hitherto has been customary. But this thorough "understanding" was not an end in itself. It was to be used especially in translating the Bible accurately and fully into such language as would make the meanings in the Bible attach to their thinking and experience.

In the sessions of the Summer Institute of Linguistics held each year at the University of Oklahoma, the University of Washington, and at the University of North Dakota, intensive courses in linguistics prepare the students to attack economically and master effectively, in contact with native speakers in the field, languages that are exceedingly complicated and structurally very different from any of the languages of the Indo-European family, to which English belongs. Under the direction of Kenneth L. Pike and his associates this language learning has been highly successful and a great number of descriptive structural analyses turned out by these workers are accepted and published in the best journals devoted to scientific linguistic studies.

Not only is the linguistic training of these workers highly productive, in their ability to learn to speak these exotic languages well, and to analyze and describe the language forms and processes with scientific acceptability, but this growing body of exact information concerning the nature and functioning of a tremendous range of very different languages has provided the basis for very significant advances in linguistic theory. Kenneth Pike's book, *Language in Relation to a Unified Theory of the Structure of Human Behavior,*[62] his "Dimensions of Grammatical Constructions,"[63] and especially his treatment of "Language as Particle, Wave, and Field"[64] plow new ground and offer new approaches to old problems.

Concerning the applications of linguistic knowledge to other fields the last chapter of Bloomfield's *Language,* 1933, presents some very brief comments.[65]

Psycholinguistics

The last quarter of a century or so has seen the development of at least two major approaches to the study of language: that represented by structural linguistics and that represented by behavioral psychology. The two have progressed more or less independently. . . . The kind of question the linguist asks is essentially one like "Does this as yet unobserved message conform to the rules of this code?" or more simply, "Can a speaker ever say this?" . . .

There are presumably some finite set of variables affecting the learning process, and the psychologist's question is something like "What factors are operating to cause this speaker to say this at this time?"

There is need for some exploration of the relationship of these two views, the structural, all-or-nothing, deterministic view on the one hand and the behavioral, more-or-less, probabilistic view on the other. It is not clear to what extent they are contradictory or merely complementary. However, it seems likely that there are gaps in each approach which make communication across disciplines not only desirable but necessary.[66]

The first formal efforts to set up "communication across" the disciplines, linguistics and psychology, resulted in the interuniversity summer research seminar held at Cornell University, June 18–August 10, 1951. The Social Science Research Council's Committee on Linguistics and Psychology was established in October 1952, with the purpose of bringing together "men trained in the various fields relating to the study of language with a view to planning and developing research on language behavior."[67] The second seminar was held at the University of Indiana in conjunction with the Linguistic Institute, during the summer of 1953. The results of the work of that seminar were published in the volume entitled *Psycholinguistics: A Survey of Theory and Research Problems,* edited by Charles E. Osgood and Thomas A. Sebeok.

Psycholinguistics is by no means a sharply defined field, but there has developed in it a great interest and vigorous activity. The selections brought together in the recent volume entitled *Psycholinguistics*[68] is a valuable and convenient collection of articles bearing upon language through which to stimulate and develop increasing communication between these disciplines.

Machine Translation

The discussion concerning the use of high-capacity general-purpose computers for the purpose of translating scientific reports has increased rapidly in volume since the suggestion was put forward in 1949.[69] By 1952 preliminary work on the problems involved was discussed both at Massachusetts Institute of Technology and at the Seventh International Congress of Linguists in London. The research in this field (referred to not only as "machine translation" but also as "mechanical translation" and "automatic translation") was reported on and discussed at the Eighth International Congress of Linguists, in Oslo in 1957.[70]

A logical machine, in order to translate, has to perform the following sets of operations: it has to read the input text in the source language, it has to manipulate the input translationally, and it has to furnish a usable output in the target language. . . .

A translation program, to be successful, has to accomplish more than merely the one-by-one transfer of units from the source language into the target language. It has to include some solution to the problems of choice implicit in the fact that (a) a unit in the source language may have more than one possible equivalent in the target language, and (b) that the order of source-language units in the input may not be suitable for the output in the target language. . . . the required selection and arrangement decisions can be programmed only if the contextual conditions can be determined under which any given decision from among several possible ones is to be implemented. The linguist's major contribution to MT research consists in the discovery of these conditions, and in the formulation of a routine for basing a decision on it.

There appears to be a certain correlation, on the one hand between lexical conditions and selection decisions, and on the other hand between syntactic conditions and arrangement decisions, but it is by no means to be assumed that selection decisions are based on lexical conditions only, nor that arrangement decisions are based on syntactic— or, more generally, grammatical—conditions only.[71]

The efforts to identify, describe, and program the linguistic cues of a text so that a computer could perform the translating operation have stimulated a variety of new approaches to linguistic analysis[72]—especially those of a mathematical-logical character. Warren Plath, of Harvard University, in his article "Mathematical Linguistics,"[73] has furnished an up-to-date survey and bibliography of the achievements in this new field of language study.

Transformations and a Generative Grammar

The linguistic approach frequently referred to as "transform grammar" seems to have arisen out of one of the attempts to deal with portions of discourse larger than the individual "sentence"— that by Zellig Harris as set forth in his articles entitled "Discourse Analysis" and "Discourse Analysis: A Sample Text."[74] The following quotations from the first article give a general statement of this new approach.

Distributional or combinatorial analysis within one discourse at a time turns out to be relevant to both of these problems.

On the one hand, it carries us past the sentence limitation of descriptive linguistics. Although we cannot state the distribution of sentences (or, in general, any inter-sentence relation) when we are given an arbitrary conglomeration of sentences in a language, we can get quite definite results about certain relations across sentence boundaries when we consider just the sentences of a particular connected discourse—that is, the sentences spoken or written in succession by one or more persons in a single situation. This restriction to connected discourse does not detract from the usefulness of the analysis, since all language occurrences are internally connected. Language does not occur in stray words or sentences, but in connected discourse—from a one-word utterance to a ten-volume work, from a monolog to a Union Square argument. Arbitrary conglomerations of sentences are indeed of no interest except as a check on grammatical description; and it is not surprising that we cannot find interdependence among the sentences of such an aggregate. The successive sentences of a connected discourse, however, offer fertile soil for the methods of descriptive linguistics, since these methods study the relative distribution of elements within a connected stretch of speech.

On the other hand, distributional analysis within one discourse at a time yields information about certain correlations of language with other behavior. The reason is that each connected discourse occurs within a particular situation—whether of a person speaking, or of a conversation, or of someone sitting down occasionally over a period of months to write a particular kind of book in a particular literary or scientific tradition. To be sure, this concurrence between situation and discourse does not mean that discourses occurring in similar situations must necessarily have certain formal characteristics in common, while discourses occurring in different situations must have certain formal differences. The concurrence between situation and discourse only makes it understandable, or possible, that such formal correlation should exist.[75]

This method "seeks to provide statements of the elements, and in particular of the relative occurrence of all the elements of a discourse within the limits of that one discourse." That is,

Elements in identical environments
Elements in equivalent environments
Equivalence classes
Sentence order

Out of this work came the understanding of "equivalent sentences"—that

. . . two otherwise different sentences contain the same combination of equivalent classes even though they may contain different combinations of morphemes. . . . If we can show that two sequences are equivalent in any English sentences in which they occur, then they are equivalent in any text written in English.

But what is "equivalence"? *Two elements* are equivalent if they occur in the same environment within the sentence. *Two sentences* in a text are equivalent simply if they both occur in the text (unless we discover structural details fine enough to show that two sentences are equivalent only if they occur in similar structural positions in the text). Similarly, two sentences in a language are equivalent if they both occur in the language. In particular, we will say that sentences of the form A are equivalent to sentences of the form B, if for each sentence A we can find a sentence B containing the same morphemes except for differences due to the difference in form between A and B. For example, $N_1 V N_2$ is equivalent to N_2 *is* V-*en by* N_1 because for any sentence like *Casals plays the cello* we can find a sentence *The cello is played by Casals*.

We do not claim that two equivalent sentences necessarily mean exactly the same thing, or that they are stylistically indifferent. But we do claim that not all sentences are equivalent in this sense: the relation of equivalence is not useless, as it would be if it were true for all sentences.[76]

But for "equivalence" of this sort the grammatical forms of the two sentences need not be alike:

> Grammatical equivalence can be investigated more systematically if we introduce a technique of experimental variation. Given a sentence in form A and a desired form B, we try to alter A by only the formal difference that exists between it and B, and see what happens then to our A. Given *The memorable concerts were recorded . . . ,* suppose that we want to make this MNR sentence comparable in form to previous intervals beginning with N. To this end, we seek a variation of the sentence beginning *The concerts.* We may do this by putting an informant into a genuine social speech situation (not a linguistic discussion about speech) in which he would utter a sentence beginning *The concerts* and containing the words *memorable* and *recorded.* Or we may do it by the tedious job of observation, hunting for a sentence that begins with *The concerts* and contains *memorable* and *recorded.* By either method, we might get *The concerts were memorable and were recorded,* or something of the sort, whence we learn that when M (or any adjective) is shifted to the other side of N (its following noun) one inserts *is;* MN is equivalent to N *is* M. In this way we discover that when MNR is shifted to a form beginning with N, an *is* appears between N and the following M.

This technique of varying the grammatical form of a sentence while keeping its morphemes constant cannot be used within a text for there all we can do is to inspect the available material. But it can be used in the language outside the text, where we have the right, as speakers, to create any social situation which might favor another speaker's uttering one rather than another of the many sentences at his disposal. It is especially useful in a language like English, where so many morphemes occur in various grammatical classes.

The preceding paragraph indicates the basic safeguard in applying grammatical equivalence to extend our textual equivalence classes.[77]

Thus given the sentence "The memorable concerts were recorded," with the structure "the memorable concerts," with modifier preceding the noun, a change to the structure, "The concerts were memorable," with the modifier following the noun and the addition of the proper form of *is,* is a permitted grammatical equivalence, because of the evidence of "experimental variation."

The process of identifying permitted grammatical "transformations" has become a very useful tool in exploring the relationships between sentences. In fact, the "transform grammar" of Harris now seems to rest upon the assumption that *all the sentences* of a language are either *kernel* sentences or *transformations* of these kernel sentences.

The kernel is the set of elementary sentences and combiners, such that all sentences of the language are obtained from one or more kernel sentences (with combiners) by means of one or more transformations. Each kernel sentence is of course a particular construction of classes, with particular members of the classes co-occurring. If many different types of construction were exemplified by the various kernel sentences, the kernel would be of no great interest, especially not of any practical interest. But kernels generally contain very few constructions; and applying transformations to these few constructions suffices to yield all the many sentence constructions of the language.[78]

"Transform grammar" provides a new approach to the old task of decomposing the structures of sentences and describing or giving rules for the "elements" of which they are composed.

. . . the kernel (including the list of combiners) is finite; all the unbounded possibilities of language are properties of the transformational operations. This is of interest because it is in general impossible to set up a reasonable grammar or description of a language that provides for its being finite. Though the sample of the language out of which the grammar is derived is of course finite, the grammar which is made to generate all the sentences of that sample will be found to generate also many other sentences, and unboundedly many sentences of unbounded length. If we were to insist on a finite language, we would have to include in our grammar several highly arbitrary and numerical conditions—saying, for example, that in a given position there are not more than three occurrences of *and* between N. Since a grammar therefore cannot help generating an unbounded language, it is desirable to have the features which yield this unboundedness separate from the rest of the grammar.

Our picture of a language, then, includes a finite number of actual kernel sentences, all cast in a small number of sentence structures built out of a few morpheme classes by means of a few constructional rules; a set of combining and introducing elements; and a set of elementary transformations, such that one or more transformations may be applied to any kernel sentence or any sequence of kernel sentences, and such that any properly transformed sentences may be added sequentially by means of the combiners.[79]

A later statement by Zellig Harris of the "transform" approach is the following.

Transformational analysis decomposes each sentence of a language into (transformed) sentences (ultimately elementary sentences) and operators (unary and connective), without residue. This means that various sections are recognized as transforms of a sentence (or the original sentence as a whole is so recognized), and that there is no part of the original sentence which is not included in one of these transformed sentences and operators on them. The process can be repeated, each transformed sentence being itself decomposed into sections which are transformed sentences, until we obtain (transformed) elementary sentences with connectives.[80]

And another by Henry Hiż, a co-worker with Zellig Harris at the University of Pennsylvania:

I am dealing here with that branch of grammar which takes a body of sentences given empirically as its starting point, which compares sentences, which arranges them in grammatically connected sets and, by pointing out their similarities and differences arrives at structures of sentences and at smaller units into which sentences are analyzable. This procedure is manifestly the reverse of a constructive or generative path in grammar where one attempts to build up sentences from more elementary constituents.

There is an effort here to present grammatical studies of a language as something open, changing, progressing. There are infinitely many batteries of transformations for a language. We change our grammar, our global view of the language, by shifting our attention from one finite set of batteries to another.[81]

If then, as the quotations above indicate, "transform" grammar provides a grammatical apparatus for the decomposition of the sentences of a language and thus a means of establishing their mutual relationships structurally, it would seem that a "generative" grammar attempts to provide a set of procedures for just the opposite process.

The fundamental aim in the linguistic analysis of a language L is to separate the *grammatical* sequences which are the sentences of L from the *ungrammatical* sequences which are not sentences of L and to study the structure of the grammatical sequences. The grammar of L will thus be a device that generates all of the grammatical sequences of L and none of the ungrammatical ones. One way to test the adequacy of a grammar proposed for L is to determine whether or not the sentences that it generates are actually grammatical, i.e., acceptable to a native speaker, etc. We can take certain steps towards providing a behavioral criterion for grammaticalness so that this test of adequacy can be carried out. For the purposes of this discussion, however, suppose that we assume intuitive knowledge of the grammatical sentences of English and ask what sort of grammar will be able to do the job of producing these in some effective and illuminating way. We thus face a familiar task of explication of some intuitive concept, in this case, the concept "grammatical in English," and more generally, the concept "grammatical."[82]

The following quotation gives a later and more precise statement.

A *generative grammar*, in the sense of [SS] [*Syntactic Structures*], is not a large collection of neatly organized examples, supplemented with comments about these examples and hints as to how to construct similar ones. Nor is it a discussion of efficient and compact notations (e.g., inventories of phonemes, morphemes, categories or construction types) in terms of which the utterances of a corpus can be represented. A generative grammar is a system of explicit rules that assign to each sequence of phones, whether of the observed corpus or not, a structural description that contains all information about how this sequence of

phones is represented on each of the several linguistic levels—in particular, information as to whether this sequence of phones is a properly
formed or *grammatical* sentence and if not, in what respects it deviates
from well-formedness. In particular, then, this grammar distinguishes a
class of perfectly well-formed (fully grammatical) sentences. It is designed, in other words, to meet what Hockett has proposed as the basic
test of significance for a grammar, namely, that it "generate any number of utterances in the language, above and beyond those observed in
advance by the analyst—new utterances most, if not all of which will
pass the test of casual acceptance by a native speaker." To Hockett's
remark I should only like to add that a grammar must not merely spec-
ify an infinite class of properly formed utterances, but must also assign
to each sequence of phones a structural description that provides a basis
for explaining how this utterance is used and understood—that provides
the structural information without which it is impossible to undertake
this further task in a serious way [221]. . . .

The investigations of generative grammar described in [SS] [*Syntactic Structures*] were motivated in part by an interest in the problem
of accounting for the ability of a speaker to produce and understand an
indefinite number of new sentences (or for that matter, to recognize
them as properly formed, or as deviating from well-formedness in one
or another respect) ([SS], p. 15), a task that he performs regularly
with great facility. A generative grammar can be regarded as an attempt
to characterize certain aspects of this ability, and a particular theory
of generative grammar is a proposal concerning its general and universal features [222]. . . .

The study of generative grammars is, however, a natural outgrowth
of traditional descriptive linguistics. Modern linguistics has, typically,
been concerned with the much narrower problem of constructing several inventories of elements in terms of which utterances can be represented, and has given little attention to the rules that generate utterances
with structural descriptions [223].[83]

As shown earlier in this chapter, the advances made by linguistic science during the past 140 years have been marked by
some specific evidence of a break-through into new ways of working
and new understanding upon which later scholars have built. Certainly the last ten years, with the new linguistic syntheses of Kenneth L. Pike's "tagmemes," built upon an immense amount of new
linguistic data and facts concerning the structures and processes of
a very wide range of natural languages, and with the results of the
new "decomposition" procedures of "kernels" and "transformations" developed by Zellig Harris; and with the "generative" gram-

mar of Noam Chomsky—these ten years have produced new ways of attacking linguistic problems and some new views that have stimulated most vigorous discussion. Whether any of these new approaches or any combination of them will actually develop into another significant break-through as "structural linguistics" did from 1925 to 1935, and furnish the essentials of the theoretical base for the linguistic studies of the next generation, cannot now be predicted.

In the discussions of those who have tried to understand these new approaches a number of fundamental questions have been raised for which adequate answers do not seem to be available in the published materials. Valid criteria for the judgments of "grammaticality" as applied to sentences are essential for a "generative" grammar. The theoretical and practical principles upon which the criteria now used depend seem hard to find. It is also difficult to determine all the criteria to be used to judge the acceptability or permission of any particular type of "transformation."

Certainly a live linguistic science will continue to push out the boundaries not only of the verified information that constitutes our knowledge of language structure and processes, but also our understanding of the nature and functioning of human language itself.

We would then define linguistics, or linguistic science as a body of knowledge and understanding concerning the nature and functioning of human language, built up out of information about the structure, the operation, and the history of a wide range of very diverse human languages by means of those techniques and procedures that have proved most successful in establishing verifiable generalizations concerning relationships among linguistic phenomena.

In this much loaded and somewhat difficult definition there are five essential features that cannot be separated, for each succeeding feature is a qualifier of what has preceded. Perhaps the following arrangement of the parts of this definition may serve to give these important features their relative prominence:

Linguistic science is
(1) *a body of knowledge and understanding*
(2) (knowledge and understanding) concerning the *nature and functioning of human language*
(3) (this knowledge and understanding) built up out of *information* about the *structure,* the *operation,* and the *history* of a *wide range of very diverse human languages*
(4) (this knowledge and understanding built up) *by means of those techniques and procedures* that have proved *most successful* in *establishing verifiable generalizations*
(5) (verifiable generalizations) concerning *relationships among linguistic phenomena.*

NOTES

1. One author writes:

The great cry is for improved communication, and yet under the pretext of being free and easy and above quibbling, those who do the most talking and writing indulge themselves in the very obscurities and ambiguities that cause the outcry. They are abetted, moreover, by another offspring of the scientific spirit, the professional student of language. In his modern embodiment the linguist takes the view that whatever occurs in anybody's speech is a fact of language and must not be tampered with, but only caught in flight and pinned on a card. This is "scientific detachment," and it has gone so far that under its influence in many schools all the categories of grammar, syntax, and rhetoric have been discarded. The modern way to learn English or a foreign language is to absorb a phrase-by-phrase enumeration of all that might conceivably be said in ordinary talk—a directory instead of a grammar. . . . The linguists themselves pay lip service to "effective" speech, approving the end while forbidding discrimination among the means.

Jacques Barzun, "English as She's Not Taught," *The Atlantic Monthly,* December 1953, p. 25.

Frivolously, the would-be scientists argued the other way, saying that democracy and their science alike called for a policy of "Hands Off." As scientists they maintained that the speech of any group is good speech for that group; as democrats and progressives they maintained that the child should not be made to feel inferior (or superior) by changing his speech. "There can . . . never be in grammar an error that is both very bad and very common." Thus spoke Charles Carpenter Fries, the theorist who engineered the demise of grammar in the American schools. Yet this doctrine and his crusade were not, as he thought, objective and detached in the spirit of science. Rather, philanthropy and egalitarianism inspired him. To teach one kind of usage, pronunciation, and grammar seemed to him tantamount to reintroducing social distinctions of the most artificial kind. Wanting the opposite gave him his first principle: Accept what comes and in time we shall have a classless speech corresponding to the usage of the most numerous.

Jacques Barzun, *House of Intellect,* New York, Harper & Row, Publishers, 1959, p. 241.

In the two quotations above Jacques Barzun (Professor of History in Columbia University and Dean of the Faculties and Provost) is wrong, in respect to the facts, in practically every statement he makes concerning "the linguist," and the single section of direct quotation he makes from me is not only taken out of context, but out of a context that develops a point of view just the opposite of the point of view he attributes to me.

The sentence Barzun quotes comes from my *Teaching of the English Language* (New York, Thomas Nelson & Sons, 1927). In the brief summary of the immediately preceding chapter, an historical survey of "The Rules of Grammar as the Measure of Language Errors," I had used as examples "It is me" and "It is you," pointing out that historically *me* and *you* were both dative-accusative forms, that the dative-accusative form *you* had displaced the earlier nominative form *ye* in "It is you" and is now completely accepted "solely because we use it in that situation," and that "obviously the rule that 'The verb *to be* takes the same case after it as is used before it' is not the final measure to be applied in this case, but must yield, as rules have always done, to the drift and development of the language." The sentence Barzun quotes comes in the very first paragraph of the next chapter in which as a means of connection with the earlier discussion I used "It is you." I wrote as follows:

> Where that usage is practically unanimous, as it is in respect to "It is you," there is no possible appeal despite any rules that may come into conflict with it. In such cases, if the rule of grammar does not harmonize with the general usage of the language it has no validity. Rules or laws of grammar are like laws of botany, or physics, or biology; they are general statements attempting to describe the ways in which language operates to express ideas, and valid only in so far as they are accurate generalizations. But the facts of usage are in all cases fundamental. If these facts are not in harmony with the rules or generalizations we have had in our grammars hitherto, then these rules must be restated and expanded to include all the facts. There can thus never be in grammar an error that is both very bad and very common. The more common it is, the nearer it comes to being the best of grammar.

But difficulties do not arise in cases where the usage is fairly unanimous. "It is you" is not a problem; but with the pronoun of the first person there is a problem because some people insist upon using "It is I," and others "It is me." The trouble arises where usage is thus divided, in those cases in which adult English-speaking people differ in their practice. Here, obviously, the appeal to usage is futile because it is the very fact of the division of usage which creates the difficulty. . . . It is probably much more sound to decide that the spontaneous usage of that large group who are carrying on the affairs of English-speaking people is the usage to be observed and to set the standard. Certainly this would seem sound as far as the teaching of the schools is concerned if we agree that education must bear directly upon and prepare for life. When, then, this usage is practically unanimous in respect to any form or construction that form or construction is correct and acceptable English grammar. When this usage differs in respect to any form or construction we must set up some other principle of decision. To do that is the purpose of the rest of this chapter. . . .

To avoid possible misunderstanding let me call attention to the fact that we are not here discussing the artistic use of language nor are we attempting to define any ideal of the highest reaches of our language in beauty and effectiveness. We are here trying to outline some practical standards of *acceptable* English. The artistic point of view will be discussed in Chapter V and the significance of differing speech habits in the various groups will be dealt with in Chapter VI.

Mr. Barzun could not possibly have read the book from which he quotes, especially Chapter V, which deals with "The Scientific and Artistic Points of View in Language" (showing that they are complementary and not conflicting), and Chapter VI, which deals with the problems of the teachers in developing in their pupils "the language habits of those we have called the socially acceptable group" (p. 137). Nor could he have looked at the first chapter of my *American English Grammar* (1940), entitled "The Social Significance of Differences in Language Practice and the Obligation of the Schools," and Chapter XI, "Some Inferences from This Study for a Workable Program in English Language for the Schools." In fact the sub-title of the book itself should provide an obvious clue for one who has any interest in discovering what I really believe concerning usage. The whole title is the following: *American English Grammar: The Grammatical Structure of Present-Day English with Especial Reference to Social Differences or Class Dialects.*

Nor could anyone attribute to me the views given in the Barzun quotations if he had looked at the introduction to my *Structure of English* (New York, Harcourt, Brace & World, Inc., 1952, pp. 3–7). The following quotation again contradicts several of Barzun's assertions.

A linguist records and studies all the actual forms and uses of the language that occur, but that recording and that study, of Vulgar English as well as Standard English, *should certainly not be taken as evidence that he therefore recommends or believes that the forms of Vulgar English can or should be substituted for the forms of Standard English.* If he is a good linguist he is very careful to note the precise areas of use in which the language forms are recorded, and he understands the problems of trying to learn to substitute the forms of one "dialect" for another. He understands, perhaps more completely than others, the nature of the task that the schools have undertaken when they assume the burden of teaching every child to use Standard English and, accordingly, he sometimes urges the limitation of that teaching to the actual forms of Standard English, as a scientific description reveals them, and the abandoning of attempts to teach forms that do not occur in the actual speech of native speakers of Standard English, forms that have become shibboleths of the classroom.

For the principles of a "linguistic" approach to the teaching of a language see my book *Teaching and Learning English as a Foreign Language* (Ann Arbor, Mich., University of Michigan Press, 1945).

Every one of these four books was published and had very wide circulation before 1953. Historically, for the influences that contributed to what Mr. Barzun calls "the demise of grammar in the American schools," I believe that Mr. Barzun must look at some of the publications giving the results of studies using educational tests and measurements, as, for example, Franklin S. Hoyt in *Teachers College Record,* VII (1906), 467–500, and some of those listed in R. L. Lyman's *Summary of Investigations Relating to Grammar, Language, and Composition,* Chicago, University of Chicago Press, 1929.

2. *Undersögelse om det gamle Nordiske eller Islandske Sprogs Oprindeke.*

3. For the details to demonstrate these two features in the beginnings of the "modern scientific study of language" see Chapter VII of Holger Pedersen, *Linguistic Science in the Nineteenth Century: Methods and Results,* Copenhagen, University of Copenhagen, 1924, trans. by John Webster Spargo, Cambridge, Mass., Harvard University Press, 1931.

4. *The Report of the Smithsonian Institution for 1863,* Washington, D.C., 1864, pp. 95–118. In England, Friedrich Max Müller delivered his "Lectures on the Science of Language" at the Royal Institution of Great Britain in 1863. His book was published in the United States in 1864.

5. William Dwight Whitney, *Language and the Study of Language: Twelve Lectures on the Principles of Linguistic Science,* New York, Charles Scribner and Co., 1867, Preface, pp. vii–viii.

6. William Dwight Whitney, *The Life and Growth of Language: An Outline of Linguistic Science,* 1875, p. 5.

7. *Ibid.,* pp. 315–316.

8. See the great mass of evidence concerning the history of one important aspect of this authoritarian approach, summarized by Andrew D. White, the first President and Professor of History of Cornell University, in *A History of the Warfare of Science with Theology,* 1895, Vol. II, Chapter XVII, 168–208, "From Babel to Comparative Philology."

9. B. Delbrück, *Introduction to the Study of Language,* trans. by E. Channing, Jena, 1880, p. 33.

10. Pedersen, *op. cit.,* p. 231.

11. Whitney, *Language and the Study of Language,* p. 5.

12. *Ibid.,* p. 6.

13. Whitney, *The Life and Growth of Language,* pp. 33–34.

14. *Ibid.,* pp. 177–178.

15. *Oxford English Dictionary,* 1888, Preface, Vol. I, v, vi.

16. See the booklet by Richard Chenevix Trench, Dean of Winchester, entitled *On Some Deficiencies In Our English Dictionaries, Being the Substance of Two Papers Read Before the Philological Society,* Nov. 5 and Nov. 19, 1857, London, John W. Parker and Son, 1857. These two papers shed considerable light upon the thinking that led the Philological Society soon after (Jan. 1858) to undertake the collection that finally made the *Oxford English Dictionary* possible.

17. See Harold B. Allen, *Samuel Johnson and the Authoritarian Principle in Linguistic Criticism,* University of Michigan doctoral dissertation, No. 1662, 1940.

18. Verner's paper was entitled *Eine Ausnahme der ersten Lautverschiebung,* referred to in English as "An Exception to the First Consonant Shift" or "Verner's Law."

19. Pedersen, *op. cit.,* p. 282.

20. *Ibid.,* p. 292, Note 1.

21. That is, spelled with *s,* but, in sound, phonetically adjusted to the character of the sound immediately preceding. After voiced sounds it is the sound [z], after voiceless sounds it is the sound [s], after the sounds [s], [z], [š], [č], [ǰ], it is a separate syllable, [ɪz], or [əz].

22. Edward Sapir, "The Status of Linguistics as a Science," *Language,* V (1929), 207, 208. Reprinted by permission. See also note by Leonard Bloomfield, attached to his article "On the Sound-System of Central Algonquian" in *Language,* I (1925), 130.

> I hope, also, to help dispose of the notion that the usual processes of linguistic change are suspended on the American continent (Meillet and Cohen, *Les langues du monde,* Paris, 1924, 9). If there exists anywhere a language in which these processes do not occur (sound-change independent of meaning, analogic change, etc.) then they will not explain the history of Indo-European or of

any other language. A principle such as the regularity of phonetic change is not of the specific tradition handed on to each new speaker of a given language, but it is either a universal trait of human speech or nothing at all, an error.

23. Whitney, *Language and the Study of Language,* p. 6.

24. See "Bibliography of Linguistic Geography," in Hans Kurath *et al., Handbook of the Linguistic Geography of New England,* Providence, R.I., Brown University, 1939, 55–61.

25. For a critical analysis of phonetic theory from the middle of the nineteenth century to 1940, see Kenneth L. Pike, *Phonetics,* Part I, Ann Arbor, Mich., University of Michigan Press, 1943, pp. 1–79. For a new constructive system of phonetic analysis, see Part II, pp. 83–156.

26. Edward Sapir, *Language,* New York, Harcourt, Brace and Co., 1921, Chapter III, "The Sounds of Language."

26a. G. B. Shaw, *Pygmalion.* Reprinted by permission of the Public Trustee and The Society of Authors.

27. See Chapter Five for a statement of some of the difficulties that arise out of interchanging the words *phonetics* and *phonics* in discussions concerning the teaching of reading. In that section I bring together and try to clarify the distinctions among the four terms *phonics, phonetics, phonemics,* and *alphabet.*

28. See the scholarly edition of *John Hart's Works* by Bror Danielsson, Stockholm, Almquist and Wiksell, 1955, pp. 117–118.

29. For further discussion of the principles and use of phonetic alphabets see the following: Charles C. Fries and Agnes C. Fries, *Foundations for English Teaching,* Tokyo, Kenkyusha Ltd., 1961, pp. 347–373 (distributed in the United States by Wahr's University Bookstore, Ann Arbor, Mich.); Leonard Bloomfield, *Language,* New York, Holt, Rinehart and Winston, Inc., 1933, pp. 86–89; Hans Kurath *et al.,* "The Phonetic Alphabet and Other Symbols Used on the Maps," Chapter IV, pp. 122–146, in *Handbook of the Linguistic Geography of New England,* Brown University, Providence, Rhode Island, 1939; Robert W. Albright, *The International Phonetic Alphabet: Its Background and Development,* Part III of Vol. 24 (1958) Number 1 of *International Journal of American Linguistics,* Indiana University Research Center.

30. See page 47 for three of the basic features of the nature of language achieved by 1875.

31. During the last ten or twelve years there has been a growing awareness of the differences between American and European linguists. Differences are to be expected and should cause no concern unless they make impossible or difficult a mutual understanding of the scientific contributions produced by either group. Europeans have had difficulty in thoroughly grasping the significance of American studies, and Americans have not given enough patient effort to understanding the European work. (See Einar Haugen, "Directions in Modern Linguistics," *Language,* XXVII [1951], 211–222.)

Achieving such mutual understanding is part of the function of the International Congress of Linguists. The volume on *Trends in American and European Linguistics,* published for the 1962 meetings of the ninth International Congress, is one step toward this goal.

32. For a list of the American Indian languages in North America and the language families to which they belong see Memoir 9 of the *International Journal of American Linguistics,* entitled *Indian Tribes of North America,* by Harold E. Driver, *et al.,* Bloomington, Ind., Indiana University Publications, 1953, 30 pages and a detailed map. Most of those who have contributed to the development of structural linguistics (through "descriptive" linguistics) in America have been either linguistic anthropologists, like Edward Sapir, Charles Hockett, Carl Voegelin, and Harry Hoijer or linguists who have spent considerable time working with Indian languages, like Leonard Bloomfield, Zellig Harris, and Kenneth Pike.

33. Leonard Bloomfield, review of Ferdinand de Saussure's *Cours de linguistique générale,* 2nd ed., 1922, in *Modern Language Journal,* VIII (1924), 318, 319.

34. Leonard Bloomfield, review of Edward Sapir's *Language,* in *The Classical Weekly,* XV (1922), 142.

35. There is still some confusion in the use of this term. There are those who regard the developments since 1925 as constituting "descriptive linguistics" in contrast with the work of the preceding hundred years which was primarily devoted to "historical linguistics." It is true that the new approach of the last thirty-five years arose in connection with the descriptive analysis of living languages—chiefly the many diverse languages of the American Indians. The term "structural linguistics" came later in an effort to name more precisely the organizing principle of the "descriptive" methods of the new approach. Some still use as interchangeable equivalents the two names "descriptive linguistics" and "structural linguistics." Many, however, have come to believe that the principles of our new "structuralism" apply to the complete range of linguistic data and they are restudying historical linguistic data in terms of the principles and techniques that arose in the new "descriptive" analyses. Moreover, older scholars have insisted that the data upon which to construct language "history" must be soundly "descriptive." In order to avoid confusion, it seems best to follow the more recent practice of using the phrase "structural linguistics" to cover the principles and methods of "structural analysis" whether applied to working with a living informant or working with ancient texts. It is the work with these techniques and methods which has unexpectedly given us a new view and understanding of the nature and functioning of human language. This "structural linguistics" then, applies to both the "descriptive linguistics" of living languages and also the "historical linguistics" of older linguistic forms. The basic difference between the two will be the nature of the evidence and the goal to be achieved. The "structuralism" of the Cercle linguistique de Prague and that of the Cercle linguistique de Copenhagen, differs in a variety of respects from that developed in the United States.

36. Sapir, *Language,* p. 57.

37. Edward Sapir, "Sound Patterns in Language," *Language,* I (1925), 42, 43, 50.

38. *Language,* II (1926), 153–164.

39. *Modern Philology,* XXV (1927), 211–230.

40. Bernard Bloch, "Leonard Bloomfield," *Language,* XXV (1949), 92.

41. Leonard Bloomfield, *Introduction to the Study of Language,* New York: Holt, Rinehart and Winston, Inc., 1914, Preface.

42. See C. C. Fries, "The Bloomfield 'School,'" in *Trends in European and American Linguistics,* Utrecht, The Netherlands; Antwerp, Belgium, Spectrum Publishers, 1961, pp. 196–224; "Meaning and Linguistic Analysis," *Language,* XXX (1954), 57–68; *The Structure of English,* 1957.

43. Sapir, *Language,* p. 234.

44. The purpose of this chapter, which seeks to give only a summary sketch of certain significant achievements of linguistic science during the last 140 years, makes it advisable to exclude extended discussion of the signals which constitute a language code. These matters will be dealt with later in the chapters specifically devoted to analyzing the reading process in the light of the linguistic knowledge of today. See especially Chapter 3, "Language Meanings and Language Signals," and Chapter 4, "The Nature of the Reading Process."

45. The representations in phonemic notation /tɪn/, /kæn/, /nat/, /nak/, identify the sequences of "sounds" (sound contrasts) which constitute the word-patterns; the ordinary letters *tin, can, knot, knock,* represent the spelling-patterns.

46. Richard Grant White, *Words and Their Uses, Past and Present,* New York, Sheldon and Company, 1872 (entered according to Act of Congress, in the year 1870, by Richard Grant White) pp. 297–298.

47. William S. Gray, *The Teaching of Reading and Writing,* Monographs on Fundamental Education X, Paris, UNESCO, 1956, p. 68.

48. A linguistic community is any group of speakers that make the "same" responses to the same set of linguistic stimuli.

49. See the increasing number of studies that seek to restudy and reinterpret historical linguistic data in terms of a "structural" approach, for example, Henry Hoenigswald, *Language Change and Linguistic Reconstruction,* Chicago, University of Chicago Press, 1960. See also other titles listed by Kenneth L. Pike and Eunice V. Pike in *Live Issues in Descriptive Linguistics,* 2nd ed., Santa Ana, Cal., Summer Institute of Linguistics, 1960, VI, 33–34.

50. Sapir, "The Status of Linguistics as a Science," p. 209. See also Harry Hoijer, "Cultural Implications of Some Navaho Linguistic Categories," *Language,* XXVII (1951), 111–120; Harry Hoijer, ed., *Language in Culture: Conference on the Interrelations of Language and Other Aspects of Culture,* Chicago, University of Chicago Press, 1954; John B. Carroll, ed., *Language Thought and Reality, Selected Writings of Benjamin Lee Whorf,* Cambridge, Mass., Massachusetts Institute of Technology, 1956; Robert

Lado, *Linguistics Across Cultures,* Ann Arbor, Mich., University of Michigan Press, 1957. For earlier statements see the following:

> The style in which we shall do our thinking, the framework of our reasonings, the matters of our subjective apprehension, the distinctions and relations to which we shall direct our chief attention, are thus determined in the main for us, not by us. In learning to speak with those about us, we learn also to think with them: their traditional habits of mind become ours. In this guidance there is therefore something of constraint, although we are little apt to realize it. Study of a foreign language brings it in some measure to our sense. He who begins to learn a tongue not his own is at first hardly aware of any incommensurability between its signs for ideas and those to which he has been accustomed. But the more intimately he comes to know it, and the more natural and familiar its use becomes to him, so much the more clearly does he see that the dress it puts upon his thoughts modifies their aspect, the more impossible does it grow to him to translate its phrases with satisfactory accuracy into his native speech. The individual is thus unable to enter into a community of language-users without some abridgment of his personal freedom—even though the penalty be wholly insignificant as compared with the accruing benefit. Thus, too, each generation feels always the leading hand, not only of the generation that immediately instructed it, but of all who have gone before, and taken a part in moulding the common speech; and, not least, of those distant ages, whose action determined the grand structural features of each tongue now spoken. Every race is, indeed, as a whole, the artificer of its own speech, and herein is manifested the sum and general effect of its capacities in this special direction of action; but many a one has felt through all the later periods of its history the constraining and laming force of a language unhappily developed in its first stages of formation; which it might have made better, had the work been to do over again, but which now weighs upon its powers with all the forces of disabling inbred habit. Both the intellectual and the historical career of a race is thus in no small degree affected by its speech.

Whitney, *Language and the Study of Language,* pp. 445–446.

> *The chief intellectual classifications that constitute the working capital of thought have been built up for us by our mother tongue.* Our very lack of explicit consciousness in using language that we are employing the intellectual systematizations of the race shows how thoroughly accustomed we have become to its logical distinctions and groupings.

John Dewey, *How We Think,* Boston, D. C. Heath and Co., 1910, p. 175.
51. Sapir, *Language,* p. 8.

52. Whitney, *The Life and Growth of Language.*

53. Fries, *The Teaching of the English Language.*

54. *Ibid.,* p. 44.

55. C. C. Fries, *The Structure of English,* New York, Harcourt, Brace & World, 1952.

56. C. C. Fries, *English Word Lists,* Washington, D.C., American Council on Education, 1940.

57. Kenneth L. Pike, *Pronunciation* (Vol. I of the three volumes of *An Intensive Course in English for Latin-American Students*), Ann Arbor, Mich., English Language Institute of the University of Michigan, 1942, pp. 25–97.

58. C. C. Fries, *The Teaching and Learning of English as a Foreign Language,* Ann Arbor, Mich., University of Michigan Press, 1945.

59. A recent article in *Language Learning,* X (1960), 67–88, Mary Jane Norris, "A List of Descriptions of Present-Day Languages," shows something of the extent of the activity in this type of exploration, and furnishes a helpful list of some of the descriptive analyses useful for further work.

60. Charles C. Fries and Agnes C. Fries, *Foundations for English Teaching,* published for the English Language Exploratory Committee, by Kenkyusha Ltd., Tokyo, 1961. (Distributed in the United States by Wahr's University Book Store, Ann Arbor, Michigan, and by the National Council of Teachers of English.)

61. In *Trends in European and American Linguistics, 1930–1960,* edited on the Occasion of the Ninth International Congress of Linguists, Utrecht, The Netherlands, Spectrum Publishers, 1961.

62. Kenneth L. Pike, *Language in Relation to a Unified Theory of the Structure of Human Behavior,* Glendale, Calif., Summer Institute of Linguistics, Part I, 1954; Part II, 1955; Part III, 1960.

63. Kenneth L. Pike, Presidential address for the Linguistic Society of America, December 28, 1961, published in *Language* XXXVIII (1962).

64. Kenneth L. Pike, "Language as Particle, Wave, and Field," *The Texas Quarterly,* II (1960) 37–54.

65. Bloomfield, *Language,* Chapter 28, "Applications and Outlook," pp. 496–509.

66. Sol Saporta, ed., *Psycholinguistics: A Book of Readings,* New York, Holt, Rinehart and Winston, Inc., 1961, Preface, p. v.

67. John W. Gardner, Foreword, in Charles E. Osgood and Thomas A. Sebeok, eds., *Psycholinguistics: A Survey of Theory and Research Problems,* Publications in Anthropology and Linguistics, Memoir 10, Bloomington, Ind., Indiana University, 1954.

68. See Note 66, above.

69. The memorandum written by Warren Weaver has been reprinted in William N. Locke and A. Donald Booth, eds., *Machine Translation of Languages,* Cambridge, Mass., The Technological Press of the Massachusetts Institute of Technology, 1955, pp. 15–23.

70. See the reports by Paul L. Garvin and Erwin Reifler in *Proceedings of the Eighth International Congress of Linguists,* Oslo, Oslo University Press, 1958, pp. 502–539.

71. *Ibid.,* pp. 503, 505–506.

72. For the many publications on various aspects of the research dealing with the linguistic problems involved, see E. Delavenay and K. Delavenay, *Bibliography of Mechanical Translation* (1959), International Study Group on Mechanical Translation, Paris, UNESCO.

73. Warren Plath, "Mathematical Linguistics," in *Trends in European and American Linguistics, 1930–1960,* pp. 21–57. See also Yuen Ren Chao, "Models in Linguistics and Models in General," in *Logic, Methodology and Philosophy of Science: Proceedings of the 1960 International Congress,* ed. by E. Nagel, P. Suppes, and A. Tarski, Stanford, Calif., Stanford University Press, 1962.

74. Zellig S. Harris, "Discourse Analysis," *Language,* XXVIII (1952), 1–30, and "Discourse Analysis: A Sample Text," *Language,* XXVIII (1952), 474–498.

Other approaches to the problems of dealing with portions of discourse larger than single "sentences" have been shown by Kenneth L. Pike. (See *Language in Relation to a Unified Theory of the Structure of Human Behavior,* Part I, 5, 63, "On Linguistic Units Larger than Sentences.") See also Fries, Chapter XI, " 'Sequence' Sentences and 'Included' Sentences," and Chapter VIII, Section III, pp. 164–172, in *The Structure of English, op. cit.*

75. Harris, "Discourse Analysis," p. 19.

76. *Ibid.*

77. *Ibid.*

78. Zellig S. Harris, "Co-occurrence and Transformation in Linguistic Structure," *Language,* XXXIII (1957), 335. See also his later publication *Strings and Transformations in Language Description,* Papers on Formal Linguistics, Number 1, Philadelphia, The University of Pennsylvania, Department of Linguistics, 1961.

79. Harris, "Co-occurrence and Transformation in Linguistic Structure," pp. 338–399.

80. Harris, *Strings and Transformations in Language Description,* p. 10.

81. Henry Hiż, "Congrammaticality, Batteries of Transformations and Grammatical Categories," in *Proceedings of the Symposia in Applied Mathematics,* Providence, American Mathematical Society, 1960, XII, 1, 13.

82. Noam Chomsky, *Syntactic Structures,* The Hague, The Netherlands, Mouton and Co., 1957, p. 13.

83. Noam Chomsky, "Some Methodological Remarks on Generative Grammar," *Word,* XVII (August 1961), 221–223. For a list of materials of transformation and generative grammar, see Noam Chomsky "On the Notion 'Rule of Grammar,' " in *Structure of Language and Its Mathematical Aspects,* Vol. XII of *Proceedings of the Symposia in Applied Mathematics,* Providence, R.I., American Mathematical Society, 1961, p. 16, n. 14.